Mighty Mentals

Book C

Peter Maher

Name ______________________________

Class ______________________________

Contents

Note to teachers and parents

Developing mental arithmetic skills

Automatic response—the ability to quickly recall basic mathematical facts, or to apply a known fact to a slightly modified situation or application—is an essential prerequisite for success in mathematics.

The development of modern technology and its applicability to the classroom in the form of the hand-held calculator has not diminished the significance of the role that mental arithmetic should play in schools. On the contrary, the advent of modern technology has increased the need for accurate mental arithmetic skill development in students. Without relatively accurate estimation prior to calculation, merely accepting at face value a solution on a screen can be fraught with danger. Inadvertently hitting the wrong buttons on a calculator is a commonly occurring fact of life. The result on the screen should never be blindly accepted. When we consider the fact that the great majority of the calculations secondary school students complete are done on the calculator, the validity of this point can be readily perceived.

By the end of primary school, a student should be in the habit of estimating and rounding off prior to using a calculator for computational purposes.

Appropriate estimation is reliant upon a sound knowledge of basic number facts, which should have been developed consistently throughout the primary years.

The better a student's abilities with mental arithmetic, the less time he or she will have to devote to looking up answers on a screen, in a book or on a chart. This point is demonstrated graphically with the game of 'beat the calculator'. Line up your students in pairs and tell them that some maths questions are going to be asked of the students who progressively come to the head of the line. Offer a calculator to one of the two students. Both will want it but only allow one to prevail. The other student will complain about how unfair the game is until the rules are made clear. The student with the calculator must press the appropriate buttons and display the correct answer. Ask the pairs of students questions they should be able to recall relatively quickly, such as 2 x 5 or 7 + 4. Now watch the student with the calculator complain that the game is unfair because the calculator is an encumbrance. Slip in the question 9 x 35 to see who is first with the correct answer. If the student using mental arithmetic is highly competent, 350 – 35 = 315 (10 lots of 35 minus one lot of 35) might still beat the calculator's 9 x 35 = 315.

It is also the case that the faster a student is with his or her basic number facts, the greater is the likelihood of structural computational success. Algorithms, such as long multiplication and division, contain numerous steps and stages. Students with inadequate mental arithmetic skills often take so long to recall a basic number fact that they forget the stage of the algorithm that they are progressing through. For these students the necessary foundation of times tables knowledge is inadequate—it is like trying to build on a foundation of sand. Without the necessary prerequisites of number facts competence, the algorithmic 'house' will tumble down.

It is invariably the case that the broader a student's body of mathematical knowledge, the more he or she will achieve in the subject and the more enjoyment that student will derive from the discipline. The message is clear: regularly practise automatic response games and activities, chants and rounds and all will benefit. Try to teach these number facts in as fun and meaningful a way as possible. Incorporate concrete materials and incentives into your number facts lessons.

Above all, teach for understanding. When teaching the 3 times table, show that the digits in the multiples will always sum to 3, 6 or 9. Show that the answers to the 9 times table always sum to 9. Show that adding on 8 is no harder than adding on 10—just jump back 2. Explain that the metric prefix 'kilo' stands for the number 1000, therefore there have to be 1000 grams in a kilogram and 1000 metres in a kilometre and, heaven forbid, 1000 tons of TNT in a kiloton bomb.

The patterns that make number-facts-recall easy are out there and easy enough to find. Make the effort to demonstrate them at every possible opportunity. This book and the other books in this series will show you how.

How to use this book

The challenge of acquiring appropriate automatic response capabilities demands a structured and planned approach in schools. Mental arithmetic skills should be developed in a systematic manner over a period of years. The program should encompass the full range of the mathematics curriculum, covering measurement and space facts, data and chance questions as well as number problems.

The four books in this series assist with the development of mental arithmetic skills in a systematic and logical manner. Each book in the series contains 32 units of work. Each unit contains six sets of questions, which can represent one set per school day with one left over for homework. Alternatively, one day per week could be devoted to the completion of the six sets.

Each exercise in the book focuses on a specific concept, such as multiplying by multiples of 10, or the properties of 2D and 3D shapes. The exercises have been set out in a logical sequence according to topic, for example times tables should be taught prior to the concept of a common multiple; the concept of one-tenth should be taught prior to the first decimal place. However, the order in which the exercises are completed can be varied to suit the needs of your students. The exercises are at their most useful when linked to the topic under review in the classroom at the time.

The **Scope and sequence** chart on the inside front cover of this book will assist you to plan for the use of this book and to make it as relevant as possible to your students' individual learning capabilities.

At the top of each unit of work there is a **tip** for the students, to help them work through the exercises in that unit. At the bottom of each unit, you will find the relevant state **outcomes**.

The **Handy maths facts** on pages 4–5 are included as useful reference material for students.

How well am I doing? on pages 6–7 affords the students the opportunity to record their scores on the unit exercises and to rate their own progress and performance.

A list of **answers** is found in the middle of each book and can be removed and stored if deemed appropriate.

The terms used in this book

The questions presented in this book utilise a wide variety of mathematical terms that are designed to reflect the structure of the discipline and to develop a student's mathematical vocabulary. Knowing, for example, that the terms 'add', 'sum', 'total' and 'altogether' all refer to the process of addition will have obvious benefits when a student has to tackle an addition problem set in context, or when problem solving.

A **Glossary** is provided on page 72 as a ready reference.

Handy Maths Facts

x or ÷

	0	1	2	3	4	5	6	7	8	9	10	11	12
0	0	0	0	0	0	0	0	0	0	0	0	0	0
1	0	1	2	3	4	5	6	7	8	9	10	11	12
2	0	2	4	6	8	10	12	14	16	18	20	22	24
3	0	3	6	9	12	15	18	21	24	27	30	33	36
4	0	4	8	12	16	20	24	28	32	36	40	44	48
5	0	5	10	15	20	25	30	35	40	45	50	55	60
6	0	6	12	18	24	30	36	42	48	54	60	66	72
7	0	7	14	21	28	35	42	49	56	63	70	77	84
8	0	8	16	24	32	40	48	56	64	72	80	88	96
9	0	9	18	27	36	45	54	63	72	81	90	99	108
10	0	10	20	30	40	50	60	70	80	90	100	110	120
11	0	11	22	33	44	55	66	77	88	99	110	121	132
12	0	12	24	36	48	60	72	84	96	108	120	132	144

Metric prefixes

milli means one thousandth (1/1000)

centi means one hundredth (1/100)

kilo means 1000

mega means 1 000 000

Metric equivalences

1 metre (m) = 1000 mm = 100 cm

1 kilometre (km) = 1000 m

1 kilogram (kg) = 1000 g

1 tonne (t) = 1000 kg

1 litre (L) = 1000 mL

Tests for divisibility

1 x	All whole numbers
2 x	Even numbers
3 x	Digits sum to 3, 6 or 9
4 x	4 divides into last 2 digits
5 x	Numbers ending in 5 or 0
6 x	Even multiples of 3
7 x	Double the unit and find the difference between this and the tens. It will equal 0, 7 or 14
8 x	8 divides into last 3 digits
9 x	Digits sum to 9
10 x	Numbers ending in 0
11 x	Subtract units from total tens to get 0 or 11
12 x	Numbers in both the 3 x and 4 x tables

Place value chart

Thousands Period			Ones Period		
hundreds	tens	units	hundreds	tens	units
4	9	3	8	1	5

Four hundred and ninety three thousand, eight hundred and fifteen

Polygons (2D Shapes)

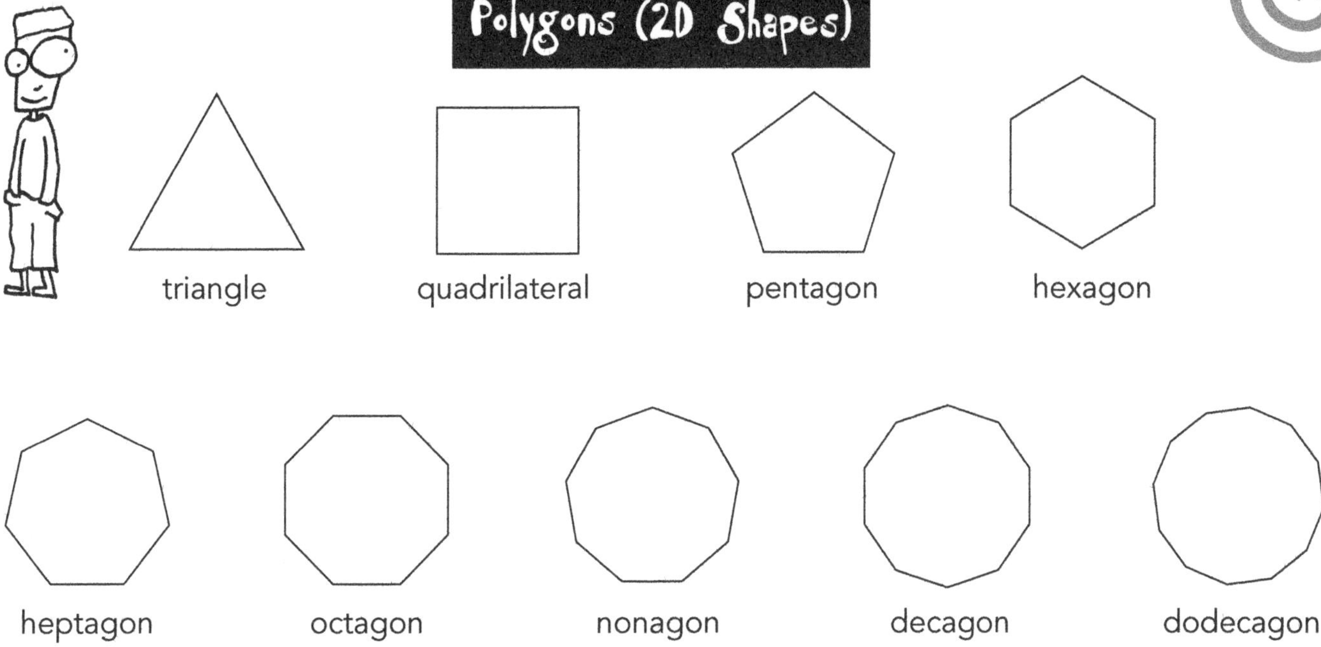

Polyhedra (3D Objects)

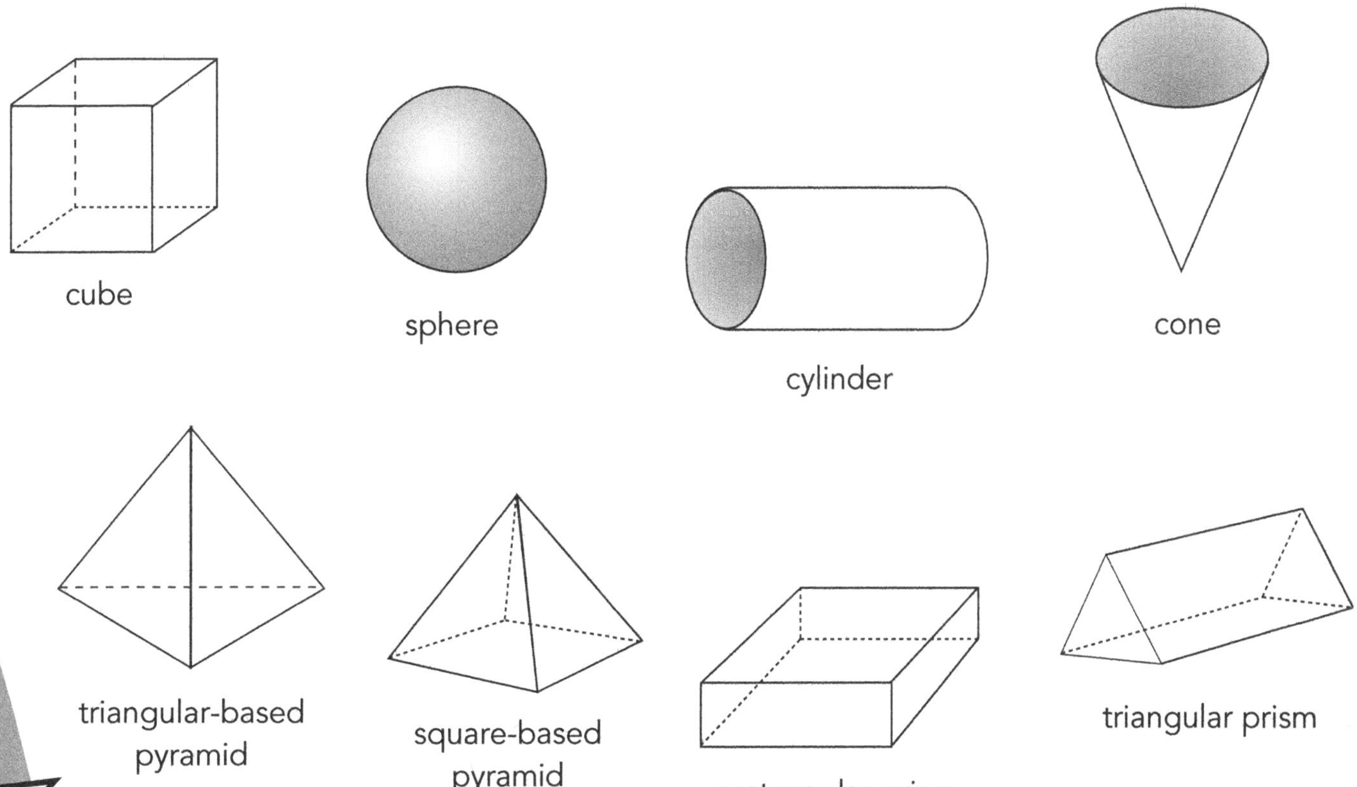

How well am I doing?

After you complete each set of work, fill in your score out of 10.
At the end of the six sets, rate yourself in the following way:

I = Can improve; E = Encouraging effort; S = Strong performer; H = Hero!

Unit	Topic	Set A	Set B	Set C	Set D	Set E	Set F	My Rating
1	**Addition:** Adding 1–20 to multiples of 10							
2	**Addition:** Adding 2-digit numbers							
3	**Subtraction:** Subtracting 1–20 from multiples of 10							
4	**Subtraction:** Subtracting 2-digit numbers							
5	**Multiplication:** The 1 times to 6 times tables							
6	**Multiplication:** The 7 times to 12 times tables							
7	**Multiplication:** Multiples of 10							
8	**Division:** Divisors of 1 to 6							
9	**Division:** Divisors of 7 to 12							
10	**Division:** Dividing multiples of 10							
11	**Multiplication:** Multiples and common multiples							
12	**Division:** Factors							
13	**Doubling**							
14	**Halving**							

Unit	Topic	Set A	Set B	Set C	Set D	Set E	Set F	My Rating
15	**Place value to 1 million**							
16	**Rounding off to 10 000**							
17	**Fractions:** Fraction of an amount							
18	**Fractions:** Equivalence and simplest form							
19	**Decimals and their fraction equivalences**							
20	**Decimals:** Addition and subtraction							
21	**Sequences**							
22	**Number strings**							
23	**Length and perimeter:** Conversions and missing sides							
24	**Area:** Concept and application							
25	**Mass:** Units and conversions							
26	**Capacity/volume:** Units and conversions							
27	**Time:** Digital and analogue conversions							
28	**Time:** Unit equivalences							
29	**Money:** Making amounts, addition and subtraction							
30	**2D and 3D:** Properties and directions							
31	**Chance:** Concepts of likelihood							
32	**Revision:** All sorts							

Number and Algebra

Unit 1 Addition: Adding 1–20 to multiples of 10

Questions like 30 + 12 are most easily done mentally, left to right.

Make the sum 30 + 10 + 2—add the tens first and then the units.

Set A

1 30 + 12 = ☐

2 40 + 14 = ☐

3 20 + 11 = ☐

4 70 + 15 = ☐

5 50 + 17 = ☐

6 80 + 17 = ☐

7 60 + 19 = ☐

8 30 + 19 = ☐

9 50 + 16 = ☐

10 80 + 18 = ☐

Set B

1 14 + 40 = ☐

2 17 + 30 = ☐

3 11 + 80 = ☐

4 19 + 20 = ☐

5 16 + 70 = ☐

6 15 + 50 = ☐

7 13 + 30 = ☐

8 18 + 60 = ☐

9 17 + 70 = ☐

10 19 + 40 = ☐

Set E

1 Find the sum of 20 and 31 _____

2 What is the total of 70 and 12? _____

3 What is the total of 40 and 11? _____

4 Add 17 to 80 _____

5 What is 13 and 40 altogether? _____

6 Find the sum of 50 and 19 and 10 _____

7 What is 30 plus 12 plus 20? _____

8 Is the total of 20, 30, 10 and 17 equal to 87? _____

9 Add 13 onto the total of 40 and 30 _____

10 Find the total of 20 and 10 and 30 and 16 _____

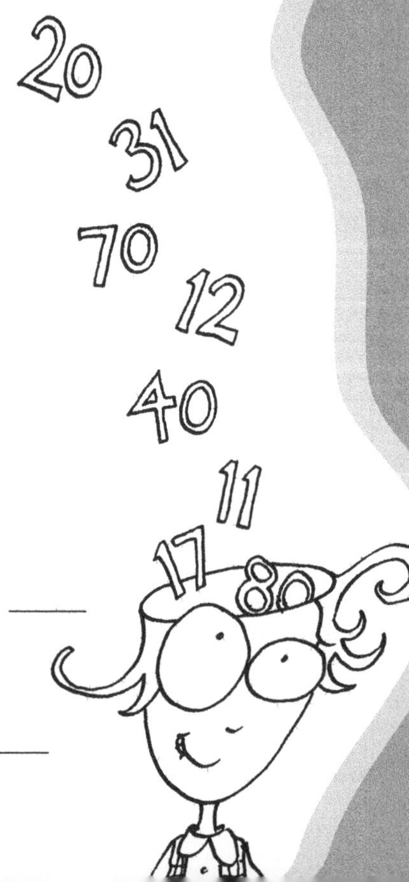

Set C

1 $10 + 10 + 14 =$ ☐

2 $10 + 20 + 13 =$ ☐

3 $20 + 20 + 18 =$ ☐

4 $20 + 40 + 18 =$ ☐

5 $30 + 20 + 11 =$ ☐

6 $50 + 30 + 16 =$ ☐

7 $40 + 40 + 12 =$ ☐

8 $30 + 40 + 17 =$ ☐

9 $70 + 10 + 12 =$ ☐

10 $20 + 40 + 18 =$ ☐

Set D

1 $18 + 20 + 20 =$ ☐

2 $11 + 30 + 40 =$ ☐

3 $17 + 20 + 30 =$ ☐

4 $12 + 30 + 50 =$ ☐

5 $19 + 60 + 10 =$ ☐

6 $15 + 20 + 20 =$ ☐

7 $18 + 30 + 30 =$ ☐

8 $13 + 10 + 60 =$ ☐

9 $16 + 40 + 40 =$ ☐

10 $11 + 50 + 20 =$ ☐

Set F

1 I had 14 basketball cards and then bought 20 more. I now have _____ cards.

2 It was 13 degrees and rose 20 more degrees to reach a top of _____ degrees.

3 Our first three batters scored 20, 15 and 40. We were 3 for _____ runs.

4 At a stud I saw 30 chestnuts, 10 greys and 14 browns. I saw _____ horses altogether.

5 In Year 5 there are 40 right- and 16 left-handers. There are _____ Year 5 students altogether.

6 My purse holds a $20 and a $50 note and $13 in change. I have $ _____ in total.

7 5X own 40 video games and 5Y own 17 games. Between them they own _____ video games.

8 In our first three netball games we scored 20, 18 and 30 goals. We have scored _____ goals in total.

9 The three rainy days this month produced 11 mm, 40 mm and 10 mm of rain: a total of _____ mm.

10 My mum owns 30 pairs of shoes and my dad 14 pairs. Between them they own _____ pairs of shoes.

Number and Algebra

Unit 2 Addition: Adding 2-digit numbers

When adding 2-digit numbers mentally, start with the tens and then add the ones, for example
32 + 44 =
30 + 40 (70) +
4 + 2 (6) = 76.

Set A

1. 22 + 17 = ☐
2. 37 + 31 = ☐
3. 54 + 33 = ☐
4. 62 + 35 = ☐
5. 71 + 22 = ☐
6. 83 + 12 = ☐
7. 45 + 33 = ☐
8. 54 + 25 = ☐
9. 22 + 61 = ☐
10. 73 + 26 = ☐

Set B

1. 17 + 61 = ☐
2. 25 + 54 = ☐
3. 37 + 62 = ☐
4. 25 + 53 = ☐
5. 12 + 86 = ☐
6. 23 + 55 = ☐
7. 31 + 45 = ☐
8. 12 + 66 = ☐
9. 32 + 51 = ☐
10. 44 + 54 = ☐

Set E

1. Find the sum of 27 and 32 _____
2. Add 52 and 44 _____
3. What is the total of 73 and 41? _____
4. 83 plus 33 equals _____
5. What is 72 and 83 altogether? _____
6. Find the sum of 53 and 55 _____
7. Add 83 and 66 together _____
8. Is the total of 64 and 41 more than 100? _____
9. 77 plus 52 equals _____
10. What is 24 and 92 altogether? _____

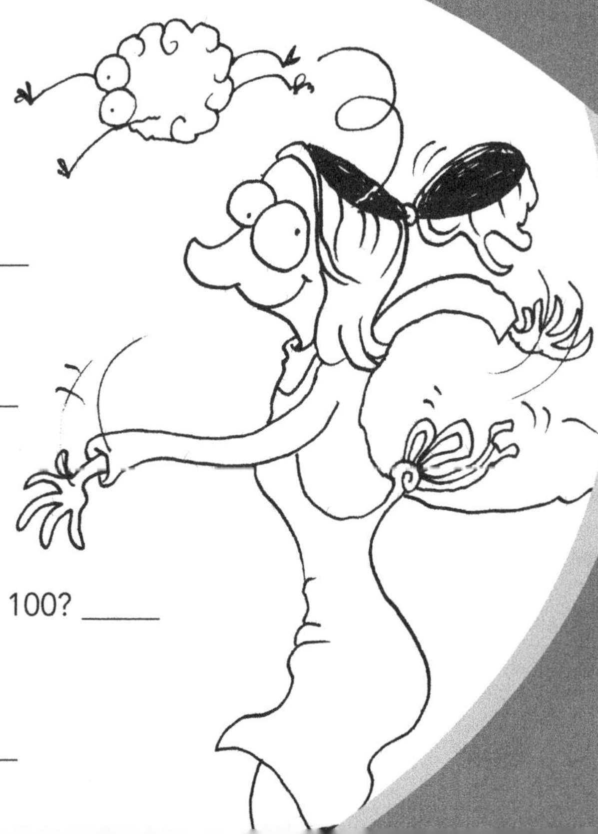

Set C

Find the sum of:

1. 65 and 42 ☐
2. 73 and 42 ☐
3. 81 and 31 ☐
4. 66 and 53 ☐
5. 83 and 54 ☐
6. 94 and 52 ☐
7. 77 and 52 ☐
8. 87 and 42 ☐
9. 68 and 41 ☐
10. 73 and 62 ☐

Set D

Find the total of:

1. 44 and 73 ☐
2. 37 and 82 ☐
3. 54 and 82 ☐
4. 27 and 91 ☐
5. 55 and 73 ☐
6. 63 and 83 ☐
7. 48 and 81 ☐
8. 27 and 81 ☐
9. 34 and 84 ☐
10. 52 and 73 ☐

Set F

1. Our openers scored 23 and 54. Between them they scored _____ runs.
2. My hand span is 15 cm and my dad's is 22 cm. Between us, we span _____ cm.
3. 5X own 23 pets and 5Y own 42 pets. The Year 5 total is _____ pets.
4. My foot is 24 cm long and my mum's is 25 cm. Together our feet stretch _____ cm.
5. Our two cars cost $57 and $32 to fill with petrol, a combined cost of $ _____.
6. The goal attack shot 33 goals and the goal shooter 54 goals. Together _____ goals were scored.
7. Our two gas bottles cost $24 and $41 to fill. Dad had to pay $ _____ to fill them both.
8. Mum drove 34 km yesterday and 75 km today. The two trips totalled _____ km.
9. My two maths books are 64 and 45 pages long, a total of _____ pages altogether.
10. The Guides sold 84 sausages today and 65 yesterday, a total of _____ sausages.

Number and Algebra

Unit 3 Subtraction: Subtracting 1–20 from multiples of 10

For questions such as 40 - 18, take the tens away first (30) and then take away the units (30 - 8 = 22).

Set A

1 40 – 14 =

2 50 – 11 =

3 80 – 15 =

4 70 – 18 =

5 30 – 17 =

6 90 – 14 =

7 50 – 12 =

8 40 – 12 =

9 60 – 11 =

10 90 – 16 =

Set B

1 3 tens – 1 ten and 6

2 7 tens – 4 tens and 4

3 9 tens – 3 tens and 8

4 8 tens – 5 tens and 2

5 4 tens – 2 tens and 8

6 5 tens – 3 tens and 7

7 6 tens – 2 tens and 9

8 8 tens – 3 tens and 6

9 7 tens – 2 tens and 8

10 9 tens – 3 tens and 7

Set E

1 What is the difference between 50 and 14? _____

2 Take 17 from 70 _____

3 90 minus 16 = _____

4 Is the difference between 60 and 14 equal to 70 – 24? _____

5 Are 50 – 11 and 70 – 31 equal differences? _____

6 Take 15 from 60 _____

7 Are 80 – 17 and 70 – 27 equal differences? _____

8 Remove 12 from 90 _____

9 Remove 18 from 50 _____

10 Reduce 70 by 13 _____

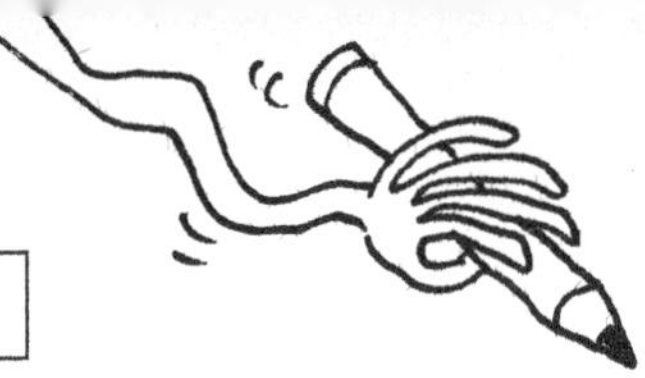

Set C

1. 50 – 10 – 10 – 4 = ☐
2. 70 – 20 – 20 – 5 = ☐
3. 80 – 40 – 20 – 7 = ☐
4. 40 – 20 – 10 – 2 = ☐
5. 60 – 30 – 10 – 4 = ☐
6. 90 – 40 – 20 – 8 = ☐
7. 50 – 10 – 20 – 5 = ☐
8. 70 – 30 – 20 – 6 = ☐
9. 50 – 20 – 10 – 3 = ☐
10. 80 – 20 – 10 – 4 = ☐

Set D

1. 6 tens – 2 tens – 12 = ☐
2. 7 tens – 2 tens – 14 = ☐
3. 9 tens – 3 tens – 13 = ☐
4. 8 tens – 4 tens – 17 = ☐
5. 6 tens – 2 tens – 15 = ☐
6. 5 tens – 2 tens – 18 = ☐
7. 8 tens – 3 tens – 11 = ☐
8. 7 tens – 4 tens – 19 = ☐
9. 6 tens – 3 tens – 11 = ☐
10. 8 tens – 3 tens – 12 = ☐

Set F

1. I had 80 swap cards and gave away 14. I now have _____ swap cards.
2. I shot for goal 50 times at training and missed on 13 occasions. I scored _____ goals.
3. 15 of the 60 children in Year 5 were ill. _____ children were at school.
4. 17 of our 60 DVDs are concerts. _____ of our DVDs are not concert discs.
5. Mum has 12 fewer smart cards than Dad. Dad has 30 cards; Mum has _____ cards.
6. Granddad weighed 90 kg and then lost 18 kg on a diet. His current weight is _____ kg.
7. My brother owns 40 CDs, 18 of which are R & B. _____ are not R & B CDs.
8. 14 of last week's 40 phone calls were for Mum. _____ calls were not for Mum.
9. 18 of the 60 points the rugby team scored came from the full back. _____ points came from the other players.
10. I ate 13 of the 50 lollies in the lolly bag. I have _____ lollies left.

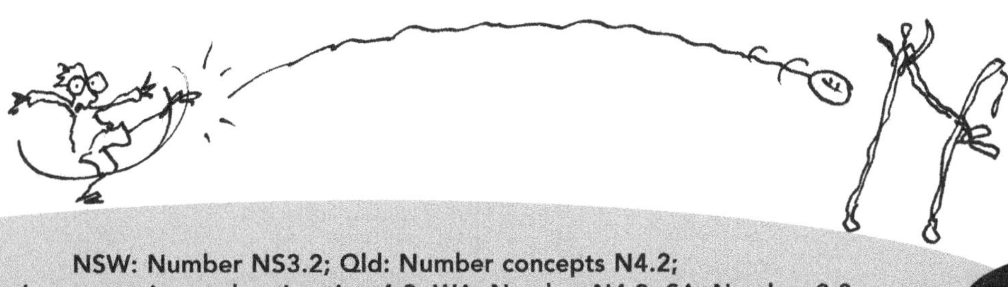

Unit 4 Subtraction: Subtracting 2-digit numbers

The best way to do questions like 87 - 52 is this: Tens first (80 - 50 = 30). Then the units (7 - 2 = 5). Then combine the two parts (30 + 5 = 35).

Set A

1 78 – 24 = ☐

2 84 – 22 = ☐

3 66 – 41 = ☐

4 98 – 36 = ☐

5 55 – 23 = ☐

6 69 – 37 = ☐

7 84 – 41 = ☐

8 75 – 52 = ☐

9 88 – 54 = ☐

10 72 – 61 = ☐

Set B

1 70 + 4 – 20 – 2 =

2 50 + 8 – 30 – 3 =

3 80 + 9 – 20 – 1 =

4 60 + 7 – 20 – 5 =

5 90 + 7 – 40 – 3 =

6 70 + 5 – 40 – 3 =

7 40 + 6 – 20 – 4 =

8 80 + 8 – 50 – 5 =

9 60 + 1 – 40 – 1 =

10 70 + 5 – 30 – 3 =

Set E

1 Remove 12 from 78 ____

2 Reduce 84 by 22 ____

3 Subtract 17 from 98 ____

4 Find the difference between 74 and 12 ____

5 Take 13 from 67 ____

6 Remove 18 from 59 ____

7 Reduce 75 by 14 ____

8 Subtract 15 from 68 ____

9 Find the difference between 77 and 11 ____

10 Take 18 from 69 ____

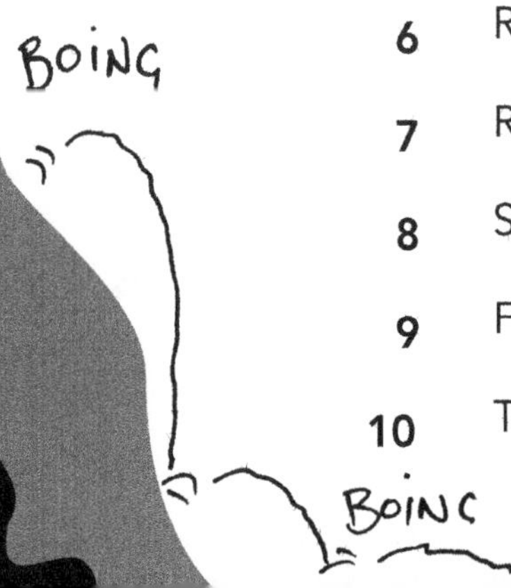

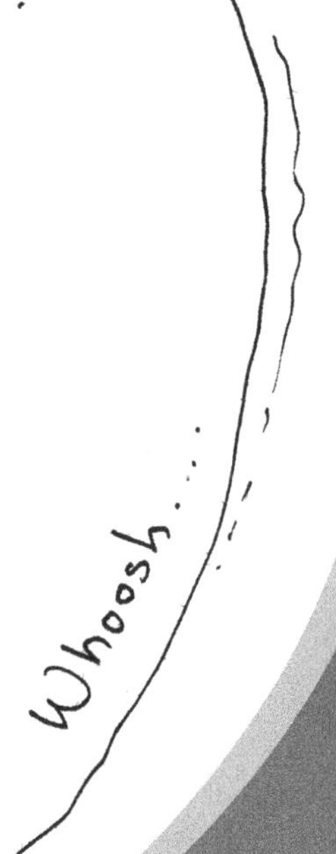

Set C

Answer 'true' or 'false' to these statements.

1 62 – 21 = 52 – 11 _______

2 78 – 54 = 68 – 44 _______

3 64 – 22 = 54 – 12 _______

4 98 – 76 = 88 – 86 _______

5 62 – 21 = 52 – 11 _______

6 94 – 72 = 84 – 62 _______

7 68 – 34 = 58 – 44 _______

8 93 – 72 = 83 – 62 _______

9 74 – 23 = 64 – 33 _______

10 99 – 55 = 89 – 65 _______

Set D

1 7 tens and 4 ones – 3 tens and 2 ones ☐

2 8 tens and 6 ones – 5 tens and 4 ones ☐

3 9 tens and 8 ones – 2 tens and 5 ones ☐

4 6 tens and 6 ones – 4 tens and 1 one ☐

5 7 tens and 4 ones – 4 tens and 3 ones ☐

6 7 tens and 5 ones – 3 tens and 5 ones ☐

7 8 tens and 5 ones – 5 tens and 4 ones ☐

8 6 tens and 9 ones – 2 tens and 3 ones ☐

9 8 tens and 8 ones – 4 tens and 7 ones ☐

10 5 tens and 8 ones – 3 tens and 5 ones ☐

Set F

1 12 of my 23 items of clothing still fit me. I will have to give away ____ items of clothing.

2 13 of our 46 tomatoes are damaged. ____ tomatoes are in good condition.

3 17 of the 98 plants in our garden are trees. ____ are other types of plants.

4 23 of the 64 squares on the chessboard are occupied by pieces. ____ squares are not occupied.

5 27 of my 88 coins are gold coins. ____ are silver coins.

6 14 of the 57 cans in the pantry are soup. ____ cans are not soup.

7 Dad blew out 36 of his 48 candles. ____ candles remained lit.

8 I used 31 of the 52 cards in the deck for a card house. ____ cards were not used.

9 17 of the 88 books in our house are sport books. ____ books are not about sport.

10 University lasts for 31 weeks a year. ____ weeks are holidays.

Number and Algebra

Unit 5 Multiplication: The 1 times to 6 times tables

Knowing that any table that uses an even number must give an even answer, like 2 x 4 or 7 x 6, might help you learn your tables.

Remember also that an odd answer will only result from an odd number x another odd number, like 5 x 9.

Set A

1. 6 x 4 = ☐
2. 7 x 3 = ☐
3. 9 x 2 = ☐
4. 11 x 5 = ☐
5. 10 x 1 = ☐
6. 6 x 6 = ☐
7. 8 x 4 = ☐
8. 9 x 3 = ☐
9. 5 x 2 = ☐
10. 6 x 5 = ☐

Set B

1. 8 x 1 = ☐
2. 4 x 6 = ☐
3. 11 x 4 = ☐
4. 3 x 3 = ☐
5. 8 x 2 = ☐
6. 4 x 5 = ☐
7. 7 x 1 = ☐
8. 5 x 6 = ☐
9. 4 x 4 = ☐
10. 12 x 3 = ☐

Set E

1. Find the product of 12 and 4 ____
2. Multiply 3 by 11 ____
3. Seven groups of 2 make ____
4. Five times twelve equals ____
5. 9 groups of 1 equal ____
6. Add 6 together 8 times ____
7. Find the product of 4 and 9 ____
8. Multiply 3 and 8 together ____
9. Twelve pairs equal ____
10. Five multiplied by itself equals ____

Set C

1 $2 \times 2 =$ ☐

2 $9 \times 5 =$ ☐

3 $4 \times 1 =$ ☐

4 $11 \times 6 =$ ☐

5 $7 \times 4 =$ ☐

6 $5 \times 3 =$ ☐

7 $3 \times 2 =$ ☐

8 $8 \times 5 =$ ☐

9 $6 \times 1 =$ ☐

10 $12 \times 6 =$ ☐

Set D

1 $4 \times 2 \times 4 =$ ☐

2 $2 \times 2 \times 3 =$ ☐

3 $10 \times 1 \times 2 =$ ☐

4 $8 \times 1 \times 5 =$ ☐

5 $6 \times 2 \times 1 =$ ☐

6 $4 \times 2 \times 6 =$ ☐

7 $4 \times 3 \times 4 =$ ☐

8 $5 \times 2 \times 3 =$ ☐

9 $6 \times 2 \times 2 =$ ☐

10 $3 \times 3 \times 5 =$ ☐

Set F

1 The 4 sporting houses in Year 5 have 10 children in each. ____ children play house sport.

2 Six 3-legged stools have ____ legs altogether.

3 10 chickens will provide ____ drumsticks to be eaten.

4 I saw 7 cars carrying 5 people each. I saw ____ people in the cars altogether.

5 The first counting number multiplied by itself equals ____.

6 Nine 6 packs of cola were bought for the party. We had ____ cans altogether.

7 The five 4s hit by the batter brought her ____ runs.

8 Last month it rained for 3 days in a row on 4 separate occasions. We had ____ rainy days.

9 Nabil had 7 pairs of pigeons; ____ birds in total.

10 Sam scored 5 out of 5 for his 10 spelling tests; a total of ____ out of ____.

Unit 6 Multiplication: The 7 times to 12 times tables

Number and Algebra

Order in multiplication doesn't matter, so once you know the 1 times to 6 times tables, you already know half the answers to the tables from 7 times to 12 times. Half the battle has already been won!

Set A

1	1 x 9 =	☐
2	5 x 11 =	☐
3	8 x 8 =	☐
4	6 x 7 =	☐
5	12 x 12 =	☐
6	3 x 10 =	☐
7	6 x 9 =	☐
8	4 x 11 =	☐
9	9 x 8 =	☐
10	2 x 7 =	☐

Set B

1	10 x 12 =	☐
2	11 x 10 =	☐
3	11 x 9 =	☐
4	8 x 11 =	☐
5	3 x 8 =	☐
6	12 x 7 =	☐
7	5 x 12 =	☐
8	7 x 10 =	☐
9	7 x 9 =	☐
10	11 x 11 =	☐

Set E

1 Find the product of 4 and 9 _____

2 7 groups of 11 = _____

3 Multiply 3 by 8 _____

4 What is 11 x 7? _____

5 6 lots of 12 equal _____

6 Multiply 10 by itself _____

7 Does 12 x 9 equal a 3-digit number? _____

8 Does 9 x 11 equal the biggest 2-digit number? _____

9 Seven groups of 8 equal _____

10 Find the product of 8 and 7 _____

Set C

1 12 x 8 = ☐

2 5 x 7 = ☐

3 7 x 12 = ☐

4 9 x 10 = ☐

5 9 x 9 = ☐

6 3 x 11 = ☐

7 5 x 9 = ☐

8 9 x 7 = ☐

9 3 x 12 = ☐

10 5 x 10 = ☐

Set D

1 5 x 2 x 9 = ☐

2 3 x 4 x 11 = ☐

3 3 x 3 x 8 = ☐

4 12 x 1 x 7 = ☐

5 2 x 4 x 12 = ☐

6 5 x 2 x 10 = ☐

7 3 x 3 x 9 = ☐

8 8 x 1 x 11 = ☐

9 1 x 3 x 8 = ☐

10 2 x 3 x 7 = ☐

Set F

1 We can make 8 teams of 9 students in Year 6. Year 6 has _____ students.

2 For 6 weeks I earned $11 for raking up the leaves. I earned $_____ altogether.

3 My 8 dogs have a total of _____ legs.

4 My birthday is in exactly 7 weeks. I must wait _____ days.

5 I collected 9 dozen eggs from the farm. I gathered _____ eggs altogether.

6 I lifted a 10 kg dumbbell six times. I lifted _____ kg doing the exercises.

7 A set of 9 tripods contains _____ legs altogether.

8 My piggy bank contains nine $5 notes. I have $_____ to spend.

9 When I turn 11, I will have lived for _____ months.

10 The 7 octopuses in the fish shop have _____ legs altogether.

NSW: Number NS3.3; Qld: Number concepts N4.3;
Vic: Mental computation and estimation 4.1; WA: Number N4.3; SA: Number 3.8

Number and Algebra

Unit 7 Multiplication: Multiples of 10

When multiplying multiples of 10, find the tables fact and add on the number of zeros in the question, e.g.
70 x 30
= 7 x 3 (21) + 00
= 2100.
This works because 10 x 10 equals 1 hundred, so 7 tens x 3 tens must equal 21 hundred.

Set A

1 30 x 7 = ☐
2 40 x 8 = ☐
3 60 x 9 = ☐
4 20 x 4 = ☐
5 90 x 6 = ☐
6 10 x 5 = ☐
7 70 x 3 = ☐
8 50 x 9 = ☐
9 30 x 6 = ☐
10 40 x 7 = ☐

Set B

1 9 x 40 = ☐
2 11 x 60 = ☐
3 8 x 20 = ☐
4 7 x 50 = ☐
5 12 x 40 = ☐
6 10 x 30 = ☐
7 8 x 90 = ☐
8 9 x 30 = ☐
9 5 x 110 = ☐
10 4 x 120 = ☐

Set E

1 Find the product of 20 and 80 ________
2 Multiply 5 by 40 ________
3 How many are 12 groups of 30? ________
4 600 times 7 equals ________
5 Find the product of 20 and 20 and 20 ________
6 Multiply 300 by 100 ___________
7 400 x 400 = 16 000. True or false? ________
8 How many are 20 groups of 20? ________
9 70 times itself equals ________
10 10 times itself times 20 equals ________

Set C

1 30 x 50 = ☐

2 20 x 80 = ☐

3 40 x 60 = ☐

4 70 x 70 = ☐

5 10 x 10 x 10 = ☐

6 50 x 40 = ☐

7 40 x 80 = ☐

8 20 x 90 = ☐

9 30 x 60 = ☐

10 60 x 60 = ☐

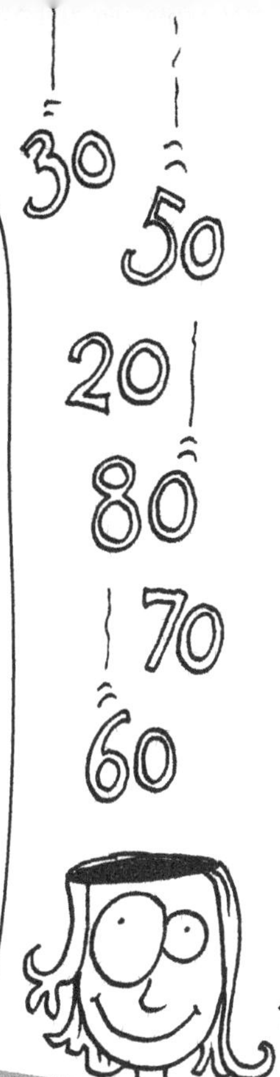

Set D

1 300 x 4 = ☐

2 7 x 500 = ☐

3 30 x 700 = ☐

4 4 x 200 = ☐

5 5 x 110 = ☐

6 120 x 7 = ☐

7 6 x 400 = ☐

8 5 x 800 = ☐

9 2 x 600 = ☐

10 800 x 9 = ☐

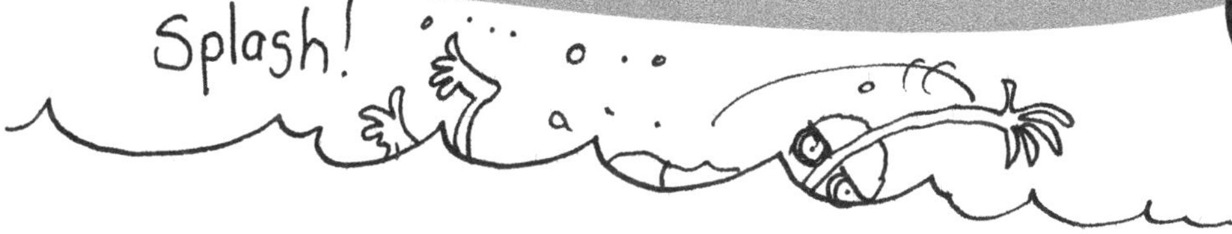

Set F

1 My five 20 cent coins are worth $ ______.

2 Olympic swimmers finish thirty 50-metre laps a day. This equals _________ metres.

3 A pack of forty 50 cent stamps costs $ ______.

4 Our school has 15 classes of 30 children or ______ children altogether.

5 Driving 400 km for 10 days will take you _________ km or from Melbourne to north Queensland.

6 Alan Border scored over 100 x 110 runs for Australia. This equals _________ runs.

7 Jack Hobbs scored one hundred hundreds playing cricket. This equals ___________ runs.

8 A grid of 40 x 40 squares would contain _________ squares altogether.

9 Thirty $20 notes would equal $ ___________.

10 Aboriginals have lived in Australia for 400 centuries. This equals ___________ years.

Unit 8
Division: Divisors of 1 to 6

Knowing your tables will enable you to divide as well. If you know that 5 x 6 = 30, you will also know that 30 ÷ 6 = 5 and that 30 ÷ 5 = 6. Divide and conquer!

Set A

1 44 ÷ 4 = ☐

2 16 ÷ 2 = ☐

3 20 ÷ 5 = ☐

4 7 ÷ 1 = ☐

5 12 ÷ 6 = ☐

6 30 ÷ 3 = ☐

7 12 ÷ 4 = ☐

8 24 ÷ 2 = ☐

9 25 ÷ 5 = ☐

10 9 ÷ 1 = ☐

Set B

1 36 ÷ 6 = ☐

2 3 ÷ 1 = ☐

3 32 ÷ 4 = ☐

4 8 ÷ 2 = ☐

5 35 ÷ 5 = ☐

6 2 ÷ 1 = ☐

7 60 ÷ 10 = ☐

8 9 ÷ 3 = ☐

9 48 ÷ 4 = ☐

10 10 ÷ 2 = ☐

Set E

1 What is the quotient of 20 and 4? ____

2 How many 2s go into 18? ____

3 Divide 30 by 5 ____

4 Divide 1 by itself ____

5 Split 48 into 6 equal pieces ____

6 12: how many 3s?

7 Find the quotient of 28 and 4 ____

8 Divide 4 by 2 ____

9 5 goes into 50 ____ times

10 42 split into 6 equal groups equals ____

Set C

1 $45 \div 5 =$ ☐

2 $6 \div 1 =$ ☐

3 $6 \div 6 =$ ☐

4 $33 \div 3 =$ ☐

5 $16 \div 4 =$ ☐

6 $14 \div 2 =$ ☐

7 $10 \div 5 =$ ☐

8 $10 \div 1 =$ ☐

9 $18 \div 6 =$ ☐

10 $36 \div 3 =$ ☐

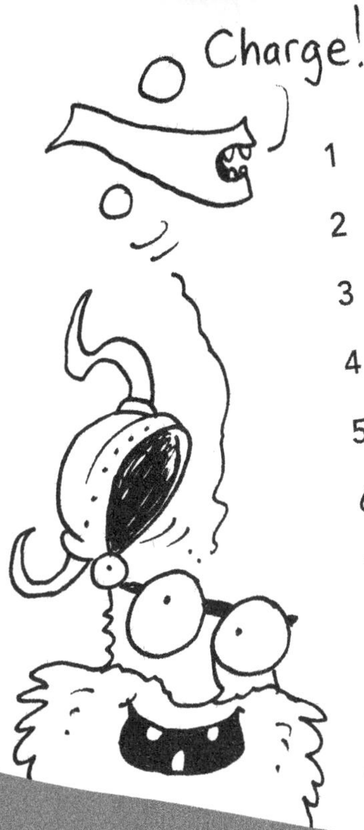

Set D

1 $45 \div 5 \div 3 =$ ☐

2 $50 \div 5 \div 1 =$ ☐

3 $36 \div 6 \div 3 =$ ☐

4 $10 \div 2 \div 5 =$ ☐

5 $30 \div 5 \div 1 =$ ☐

6 $24 \div 2 \div 3 =$ ☐

7 $12 \div 2 \div 2 =$ ☐

8 $72 \div 6 \div 6 =$ ☐

9 $60 \div 5 \div 4 =$ ☐

10 $42 \div 6 \div 1 =$ ☐

Set F

1 24 lollies were shared among 6 friends. They received ____ lollies each.

2 The 24 points we scored in basketball were all 3 pointers. We scored ____ 3 pointers.

3 36 sides are on ____ rectangles.

4 We have 12 children at school who are twins. We have ____ sets of twins at school.

5 The 55 children in Year 5 were put into 5 teams, with ____ children in each team.

6 72 eggs were packed into half-dozen sets. There were ____ sets altogether.

7 18 cricket stumps equal ____ sets of stumps.

8 I ate my 12 Easter eggs at a rate of 3 per day. They lasted me for ____ days.

9 20 children paired up. There were ____ pairs of children.

10 40 fingers are on ____ hands.

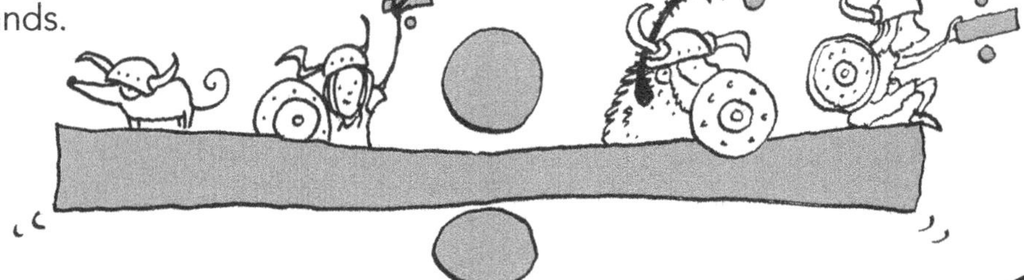

Number and Algebra

Unit 9
Division: Divisors of 7 to 12

Remember that if you know that $8 \times 9 = 72$, two division facts are now available to you: $72 \div 8 = 9$ and $72 \div 9 = 8$. Those who can multiply can also divide.

Set A

1 $54 \div 9 =$ ☐
2 $63 \div 7 =$ ☐
3 $24 \div 12 =$ ☐
4 $120 \div 10 =$ ☐
5 $32 \div 8 =$ ☐
6 $88 \div 11 =$ ☐
7 $99 \div 9 =$ ☐
8 $7 \div 7 =$ ☐
9 $60 \div 12 =$ ☐
10 $30 \div 10 =$ ☐

Set B

1 $80 \div 8 =$ ☐
2 $77 \div 11 =$ ☐
3 $81 \div 9 =$ ☐
4 $14 \div 7 =$ ☐
5 $144 \div 12 =$ ☐
6 $40 \div 10 =$ ☐
7 $64 \div 8 =$ ☐
8 $121 \div 11 =$ ☐
9 $9 \div 9 =$ ☐
10 $35 \div 7 =$ ☐

Set E

1 Find the quotient of 45 and 9 ____
2 Divide 21 by 7 ____
3 120: how many twelves? ____
4 70 equals ____ groups of 10
5 48 split into 8 equal groups equals ____
6 22 divided by 11 equals ____
7 Find the quotient of 108 and 9 ____
8 Divide 28 by 7 ____
9 96: how many twelves? ____
10 110 equals ____ groups of 10

Set C

1 $36 \div 12 =$ ☐

2 $100 \div 10 =$ ☐

3 $56 \div 8 =$ ☐

4 $66 \div 11 =$ ☐

5 $18 \div 9 =$ ☐

6 $84 \div 7 =$ ☐

7 $48 \div 12 =$ ☐

8 $80 \div 10 =$ ☐

9 $88 \div 8 =$ ☐

10 $11 \div 11 =$ ☐

Set D

1 $144 \div 12 \div 3 =$ ☐

2 $56 \div 7 \div 2 =$ ☐

3 $64 \div 8 \div 4 =$ ☐

4 $120 \div 10 \div 3 =$ ☐

5 $81 \div 9 \div 3 =$ ☐

6 $66 \div 11 \div 6 =$ ☐

7 $40 \div 8 \div 1 =$ ☐

8 $80 \div 8 \div 2 =$ ☐

9 $84 \div 7 \div 12 =$ ☐

10 $99 \div 11 \div 3 =$ ☐

Set F

1 63 fish were put into 9 tanks containing _____ fish each.

2 It was sunny for 42 days in a row. This equals _____ sunny weeks.

3 24 biscuits were packed into _____ boxes, each containing 12 biscuits.

4 A 90 cm ribbon can be cut into ________ 10 cm strips.

5 24 sides are on _____ octagons.

6 I have 110 songs on _____ CDs, each containing 11 songs.

7 __ children shared 90 lollies so that they each received 10 lollies.

8 49 basketballers can make _____ teams of 7.

9 96 apples were put into _____ bags, each containing a dozen apples.

10 55 Year 2 children were placed into _____ teams of 11 for tabloid sports.

Number and Algebra

Unit 10
Division: Dividing multiples of 10

Because division is the opposite of multiplication, dividing a multiple of 10 is the opposite of multiplying a multiple of 10.
For 150 ÷ 5, find the division fact (15 ÷ 5 = 3) and add on the zero.
For 150 ÷ 50, do 15 ÷ 5, then subtract the zeros.
The answer is 3.

Set A

1 150 ÷ 5 =
2 90 ÷ 3 =
3 420 ÷ 6 =
4 240 ÷ 2 =
5 280 ÷ 4 =
6 350 ÷ 5 =
7 240 ÷ 3 =
8 180 ÷ 6 =
9 160 ÷ 2 =
10 160 ÷ 4 =

Set B

1 210 ÷ 7 =
2 360 ÷ 12 =
3 720 ÷ 9 =
4 480 ÷ 8 =
5 660 ÷ 11 =
6 490 ÷ 7 =
7 600 ÷ 12 =
8 180 ÷ 9 =
9 240 ÷ 8 =
10 880 ÷ 11 =

Set E

1 Find the quotient of 200 and 20 _____
2 How many 7s go into 210? _____
3 Split 150 into 3 equal groups _____
4 Divide 180 by 90 _____
5 How many groups of 40 go into 160? _____
6 Find the quotient of 5 and 200 _____
7 How many 6s go into 180? _____
8 Split 770 into 11 equal groups _____
9 Divide 220 by 2 _____
10 How many groups of 8 go into 320? _____

Set C

1 $400 \div 50 =$ ☐

2 $240 \div 30 =$ ☐

3 $120 \div 60 =$ ☐

4 $180 \div 20 =$ ☐

5 $160 \div 40 =$ ☐

6 $140 \div 70 =$ ☐

7 $840 \div 120 =$ ☐

8 $540 \div 90 =$ ☐

9 $320 \div 80 =$ ☐

10 $990 \div 110 =$ ☐

Set D

1 $120 \div 6 \div 2 =$ ☐

2 $120 \div 12 \div 5 =$ ☐

3 $240 \div 3 \div 10 =$ ☐

4 $100 \div 2 \div 5 =$ ☐

5 $160 \div 4 \div 4 =$ ☐

6 $150 \div 5 \div 6 =$ ☐

7 $140 \div 7 \div 10 =$ ☐

8 $200 \div 10 \div 5 =$ ☐

9 $300 \div 6 \div 5 =$ ☐

10 $180 \div 6 \div 10 =$ ☐

Set F

1 I have $2.40 in 20 cent coins. I have __________ 20 cent coins.

2 I have $6.00 in 50 cent coins. I have __________ 50 cent coins.

3 How many $2 coins equal $240? _____

4 How many $5 notes equal $550? _____

5 How many periods of 30 days are in 330 days? _____

6 How many trips of 20 km will I need to take to travel 400 km? _____

7 There are 270 children in the school divided into _____ classes of 30 students.

8 640 kg of potatoes will be in _____ bags, each weighing 8 kg.

9 120 L of milk will pour into _____ 2 L bottles.

10 80 runs in cricket, all scored in 4s, means _____ boundaries have been struck.

Number and Algebra

Unit 11 Multiplication: Multiples and common multiples

Multiples are very similar to tables. The third multiple of 11 is 33 because $3 \times 11 = 33$. A common multiple of two numbers will be found in both their tables. For example, a common multiple of 3 and 4 is 12.

Set A

Which table has these numbers as multiples?

1 3, 6, 9 ______________

2 8, 16, 24 ______________

3 30, 35, 50, 60 ______________

4 63, 72, 108 ______________

5 77, 99, 121 ______________

6 22, 28, 32 ______________

7 7, 11, 19 ______________

8 144, 60, 48 ______________

9 24, 32, 44 ______________

10 77, 28, 84 ______________

Set B

What is the 8th multiple of:

1	7?	
2	11?	
3	4?	
4	9?	
5	5?	
6	12?	
7	10?	
8	6?	
9	8?	
10	3?	

Set E

Find the lowest common multiple of:

1 2 and 4 ____

2 3 and 6 ____

3 3 and 5 ____

4 4 and 3 ____

5 2 and 10 ____

6 4 and 5 ____

7 4 and 8 ____

8 5 and 10 ____

9 7 and 8 ____

10 3 and 9 ____

Set C

What are the 5th and the 12th multiples of:

1 7? ____ and ____
2 2? ____ and ____
3 9? ____ and ____
4 11? ____ and ____
5 4? ____ and ____
6 8? ____ and ____
7 5? ____ and ____
8 12? ____ and ____
9 6? ____ and ____
10 3? ____ and ____

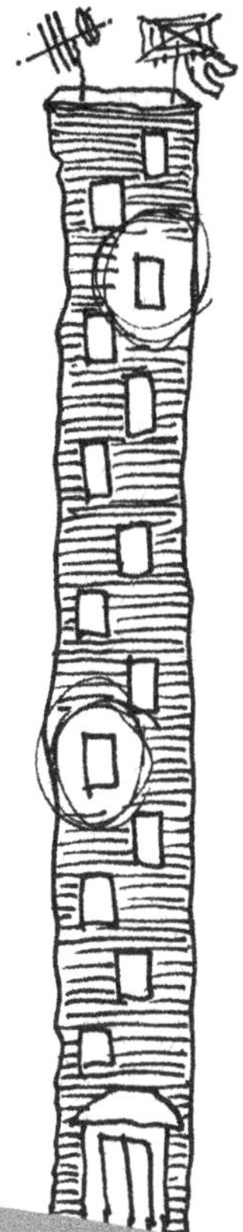

Set D

Which multiple does not belong?

1 3 ,12, 22, 30 ☐
2 8, 16, 29, 32 ☐
3 20, 30, 45, 41 ☐
4 36, 50, 132, 144 ☐
5 14, 22, 35, 49 ☐
6 81, 27, 59, 72 ☐
7 24, 10, 7, 18 ☐
8 72, 32, 48, 6 ☐
9 110, 85, 30, 120 ☐
10 19, 28, 56, 84 ☐

Set F

1 What is two more than the 3rd multiple of 11? _____
2 What is the first common number in both the 4 and 6 times tables? _____
3 The 2nd multiple of 12 equals the 3rd multiple of _____.
4 The 2nd multiple of 8 equals the _____ multiple of 4.
5 Double the tenth multiple of 3 _____
6 What is the 2nd common multiple of 2 and 5? _____
7 Is 27 a multiple of both 9 and 7? _____
8 Is 30 a multiple of both 6 and 10? _____
9 Is 22 a multiple of either 11 or 4? _____
10 What is the closest multiple of 8 to 43? _____

Unit 12 Division: Factors

A number's factors divide exactly into the number without a remainder. The factors of 6 are 1, 2, 3 and 6 because they all divide into 6. Numbers like 6 and 8 have common factors of 1 and 2. Numbers with just two factors are called prime numbers.

Set A

Which numbers have the following factors?

1 1, 2 and 4 ☐
2 1 and 3 ☐
3 1, 2, 3 and 6 ☐
4 7 and 1 ☐
5 2, 8, 4 and 1 ☐
6 10, 2, 5 and 1 ☐
7 5, 25 and 1 ☐
8 9, 1 and 3 ☐
9 8, 4, 16, 2 and 1 ☐
10 11, 33, 1 and 3 ☐

Set B

List the factors of:

1 5 ____________
2 18 ____________
3 24 ____________
4 22 ____________
5 14 ____________
6 9 ____________
7 8 ____________
8 11 ____________
9 16 ____________
10 21 ____________

Set E

What are the highest common factors of these numbers?

1 6 and 12 ____
2 2 and 8 ____
3 3 and 9 ____
4 10 and 15 ____
5 4 and 6 ____
6 3 and 12 ____
7 8 and 12 ____
8 5 and 12 ____
9 8 and 20 ____
10 20 and 50 ____

Set C

What is the second-highest factor of:

1 12? ☐
2 3? ☐
3 4? ☐
4 13? ☐
5 17? ☐
6 16? ☐
7 8? ☐
8 14? ☐
9 15? ☐
10 24? ☐

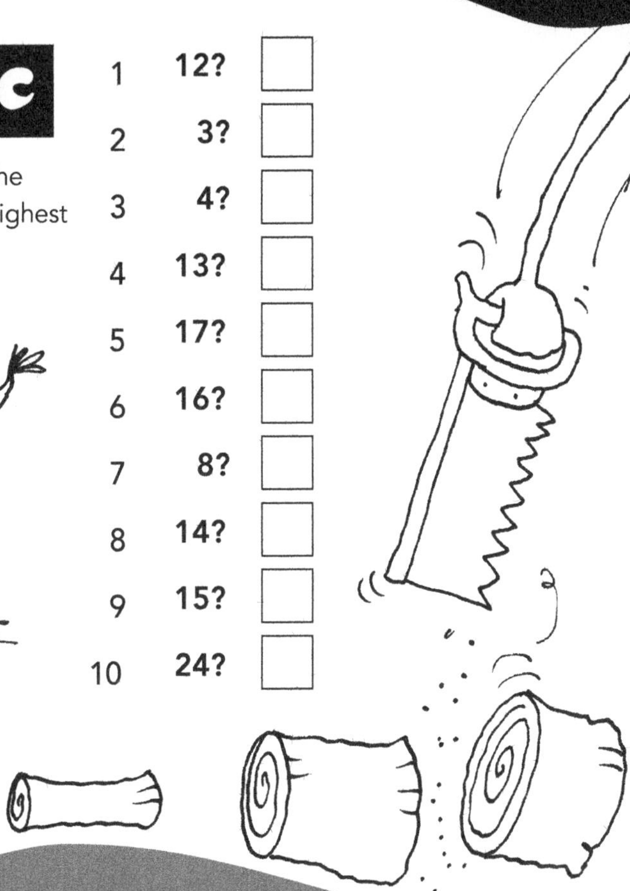

Set D

Are these numbers prime?

1 6 _____
2 9 _____
3 7 _____
4 11 _____
5 21 _____
6 13 _____
7 31 _____
8 27 _____
9 25 _____
10 23 _____

Set F

1 Is 7 a factor of 28? _____
2 Is 12 a factor of 100? _____
3 Is 8 a factor of 32? _____
4 Are both 2 and 4 factors of 16? _____
5 Are both 5 and 12 factors of 45? _____
6 What is the smallest factor of 60? _____
7 What is the highest factor of 60? _____
8 What is the second-highest factor of 60? _____
9 Is 15 a factor of 60? _____
10 Does 60 have more than eight factors? _____

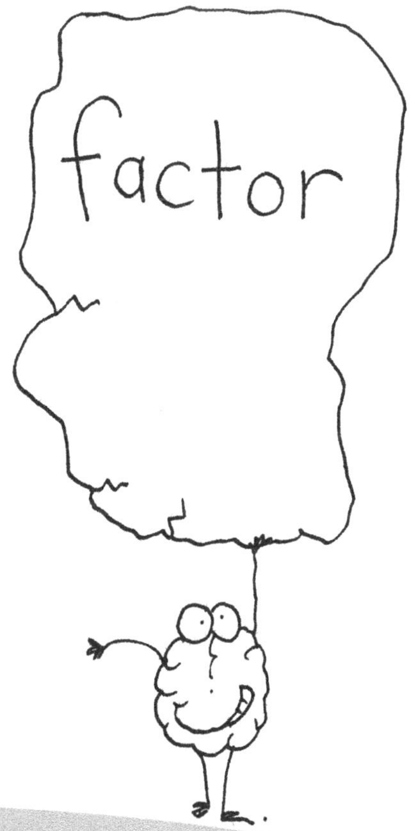

Unit 13 Doubling

When a 2- or 3-digit number is doubled, start at the left digit and move progressively to the right. For example, to double 364, do 600 + 120 + 8 = 728. To help with the adding up, you could think of 120 as being 100 + 20.

Set A

Double the numbers.

1	24	
2	41	
3	33	
4	43	
5	22	
6	13	
7	32	
8	21	
9	14	
10	34	

Set B

Double the numbers.

1	27	
2	48	
3	19	
4	35	
5	29	
6	46	
7	15	
8	37	
9	25	
10	45	

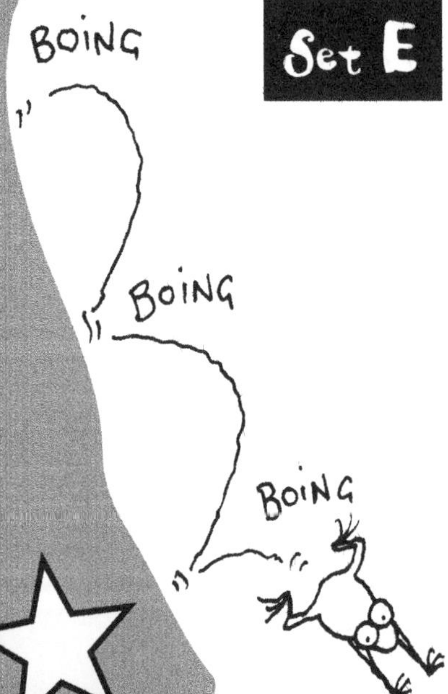

Set E

1. Double 17 ______
2. Add 135 to itself ______
3. What is 237 times 2? ______
4. Find the product of 333 and 2 ______
5. Multiply 77 by 2 ______
6. Double 134 ______
7. Add 451 to itself ______
8. What is twice 344? ______
9. Find the product of 462 and 2 ______
10. Multiply 2 by 328 ______

Set C

Double the numbers.

1. 124 ☐
2. 232 ☐
3. 331 ☐
4. 443 ☐
5. 436 ☐
6. 249 ☐
7. 326 ☐
8. 417 ☐
9. 238 ☐
10. 448 ☐

Set D

Double the numbers.

1. 362 ☐
2. 451 ☐
3. 282 ☐
4. 473 ☐
5. 181 ☐
6. 390 ☐
7. 264 ☐
8. 194 ☐
9. 350 ☐
10. 482 ☐

Set F

1. I had 28 footy cards and Sam had twice this total. Sam had ______ footy cards.
2. We were all out for 125 but our opponents scored twice as many runs, ______ runs in total.
3. In 1960, 247 people lived in our town. The population has now doubled to ______ people.
4. My 17 pet mice have doubled in number this week. I now have ______ pet mice.
5. Yesterday's 37 mm of rain has doubled this month's total to ______ mm.
6. I counted 172 cars in a car park survey both today and yesterday: ______ cars in total.
7. My friend and I have each seen 47 movies this year. We have seen ______ movies between us.
8. The Squids scored 38 points but we doubled their score. We scored ______ points.
9. We drove 472 km today and have this distance still to travel. Our destination is ______ km from home.
10. Sara's wage of $6.45 per hour will double when she is 21. Then Sara will earn $ ______ per hour.

Number and Algebra

Unit 14 Halving

Because halving is the opposite of doubling, the method for halving is the opposite to the method for doubling.

To halve 234, halve 200 (100), halve 30 (15) and halve 4 (2). Then add the three answers together to get 117.

Set A

Halve the numbers.

1 48 ☐
2 26 ☐
3 86 ☐
4 44 ☐
5 62 ☐
6 80 ☐
7 22 ☐
8 68 ☐
9 40 ☐
10 66 ☐

Set B

Halve the numbers.

1 27 ☐
2 55 ☐
3 83 ☐
4 72 ☐
5 49 ☐
6 99 ☐
7 38 ☐
8 73 ☐
9 59 ☐
10 23 ☐

Set E

1 Halve 222 _____
2 Divide 486 by 2 _____
3 What is the quotient of 881 and 2? _______
4 Split 388 into two equal groups _____
5 Half of any odd number will have a remainder. True or false? ________
6 Half of any even number will always be an even number. True or false? ________
7 Half of any even number must be odd. True or false? ________
8 Find half of 121 _____
9 Split 743 into 2 equal groups _______
10 Find the quotient of 999 and 2 _______

Set C

Halve the numbers.

1	424	
2	864	
3	226	
4	843	
5	821	
6	447	
7	625	
8	281	
9	689	
10	485	

Set D

Halve the numbers.

1	832	
2	894	
3	876	
4	694	
5	634	
6	656	
7	454	
8	470	
9	292	
10	234	

Set F

1 I spent half of my $248 at the shoe shop. I had $ ______ left.

2 I bought shoes at a half-price sale, normally costing $56. I only paid $ ______.

3 Of the $27 I paid for lunch, half was for a steak. The steak cost $ ______.

4 I live 34 km from the shops. I stopped halfway for petrol. I was then ______ km from home.

5 I watched a DVD, which lasts for 92 minutes, and stopped it halfway after ______ minutes for a drink.

6 Halfway through June is at the end of the ______ th day.

7 Halfway through a 3 hour and 10 minute game is after ______ minutes.

8 I lost half of my 188 marbles playing follow the leader. I only had ______ marbles left.

9 There are 33 levels in my new game. I am halfway through it when playing level ______.

10 The middle day of August is August the ______ th.

Number and Algebra

Unit 15
place value to 1 million

We all know that our counting or numeration system is based on the number 10 because we have 10 fingers. The place-value chart showing units, tens, hundreds of ones, followed by units, tens, hundreds of thousands is a great help when dealing with place-value questions. Use the place-value chart on page 4 of this book when answering these questions.

Set A

What is the 3 worth in the following numbers?

1 2315 ______
2 3789 ______
3 1563 ______
4 8931 ______
5 3777 ______
6 23 890 ______
7 3801 ______
8 6538 ______
9 8893 ______
10 7031 ______

Set B

What is the 7 worth in the following numbers?

1 279 490 ______
2 88 723 ______
3 72 109 ______
4 25 997 ______
5 43 975 ______
6 71 213 ______
7 80 733 ______
8 90 371 ______
9 38 795 ______
10 12 897 ______

Set E

1 How many zeros are in the number ten thousand? ____
2 How many zeros are in the number one million? ____
3 How many zeros are in the number one hundred thousand? ____
4 How many zeros are in the number twenty five thousand? ____
5 How many zeros are in the number eight hundred thousand? ____
6 Between which two digits does the space (or comma) go in the number eighty-seven thousand and twenty? ________________
7 Between which two digits does the space (or comma) go in the number four hundred and sixty thousand nine hundred? ________________

8 How many digits in the number forty thousand? ____
9 How many digits in the number six hundred thousand? ____
10 How many times bigger is 1 000 000 than 10 000? ____

Answers

Unit 1 Addition: Adding 1–20 to multiples of 10

	Set A	Set B	Set C	Set D	Set E	Set F
1	42	54	34	58	51	34
2	54	47	43	81	82	33
3	31	91	58	67	51	75
4	85	39	78	92	97	54
5	67	86	61	89	53	56
6	97	65	96	55	79	$83
7	79	43	92	78	62	57
8	49	78	87	83	no	68
9	66	87	92	96	83	61
10	98	59	78	81	76	44

Unit 2 Addition: Adding 2-digit numbers

	Set A	Set B	Set C	Set D	Set E	Set F
1	39	78	107	117	59	77
2	68	79	115	119	96	37
3	87	99	112	136	114	65
4	97	78	119	118	116	49
5	93	98	137	128	155	$89
6	95	78	146	146	108	87
7	78	76	129	129	149	$65
8	79	78	129	108	yes	109
9	83	83	109	118	129	109
10	99	98	135	125	116	149

Unit 3 Subtraction: Subtracting 1–20 from multiples of 10

	Set A	Set B	Set C	Set D	Set E	Set F
1	26	14	26	28	36	66
2	39	26	25	36	53	37
3	65	52	13	47	74	45
4	52	28	8	23	yes	43
5	13	12	16	25	yes	18
6	76	13	22	12	45	72
7	38	31	15	39	no	22
8	28	44	14	11	78	26
9	49	42	17	19	32	42
10	74	53	46	38	57	37

Unit 4 Subtraction: Subtracting 2-digit numbers

	Set A	Set B	Set C	Set D	Set E	Set F
1	54	52	true	42	66	11
2	62	25	true	32	62	33
3	25	68	true	73	81	81
4	62	42	false	25	62	41
5	32	54	true	31	54	61
6	32	32	true	40	41	43
7	43	22	false	31	61	12
8	23	33	true	46	53	21
9	34	20	false	41	66	71
10	11	42	false	23	51	21

Answers

Unit 5 Multiplication: The 1 times to 6 times tables

	Set A	Set B	Set C	Set D	Set E	Set F
1	24	8	4	32	48	40
2	21	24	45	12	33	18
3	18	44	4	20	14	20
4	55	9	66	40	60	35
5	10	16	28	12	9	1
6	36	20	15	48	48	54
7	32	7	6	48	36	20
8	27	30	40	30	24	12
9	10	16	6	24	24	14
10	30	36	72	45	25	50 out of 50

Unit 6 Multiplication: The 7 times to 12 times tables

	Set A	Set B	Set C	Set D	Set E	Set F
1	9	120	96	90	36	72
2	55	110	35	132	77	$66
3	64	99	84	72	24	32
4	42	88	90	84	77	49
5	144	24	81	96	72	108
6	30	84	33	100	100	60
7	54	60	45	81	yes	27
8	44	70	63	88	yes	$45
9	72	63	36	24	56	132
10	14	121	50	42	56	56

Unit 7 Multiplication: Multiples of 10

	Set A	Set B	Set C	Set D	Set E	Set F
1	210	360	1500	1200	1600	$1
2	320	660	1600	3500	200	1500
3	540	160	2400	21 000	360	$20
4	80	350	4900	800	4200	450
5	540	480	1000	550	8000	4000
6	50	300	2000	840	30 000	11 000
7	210	720	3200	2400	false	10 000
8	450	270	1800	4000	400	1600
9	180	550	1800	1200	4900	$600
10	280	480	3600	7200	2000	40 000

Unit 8 Division: Divisors of 1 to 6

	Set A	Set B	Set C	Set D	Set E	Set F
1	11	6	9	3	5	4
2	8	3	6	10	9	8
3	4	8	1	2	6	9
4	7	4	11	1	1	6
5	2	7	4	6	8	11
6	10	2	7	4	4	12
7	3	6	2	3	7	6
8	12	3	10	2	2	4
9	5	12	3	3	10	10
10	9	5	12	7	7	8

Unit 9 Division: Divisors of 7 to 12

Set A	Set B	Set C	Set D	Set E	Set F
1 6	1 10	1 3	1 4	1 5	1 7
2 9	2 7	2 10	2 4	2 3	2 6
3 2	3 9	3 7	3 2	3 10	3 2
4 12	4 2	4 6	4 4	4 7	4 nine
5 4	5 12	5 2	5 3	5 6	5 3
6 8	6 4	6 12	6 1	6 2	6 10
7 11	7 8	7 4	7 5	7 12	7 9
8 1	8 11	8 8	8 5	8 4	8 7
9 5	9 1	9 11	9 1	9 8	9 8
10 3	10 5	10 1	10 3	10 11	10 5

Unit 10 Division: Dividing multiples of 10

Set A	Set B	Set C	Set D	Set E	Set F
1 30	1 30	1 8	1 10	1 10	1 twelve
2 30	2 30	2 8	2 2	2 30	2 twelve
3 70	3 80	3 2	3 8	3 50	3 120
4 120	4 60	4 9	4 10	4 2	4 110
5 70	5 60	5 4	5 10	5 4	5 11
6 70	6 70	6 2	6 5	6 40	6 20
7 80	7 50	7 7	7 2	7 30	7 9
8 30	8 20	8 6	8 4	8 70	8 80
9 80	9 30	9 4	9 10	9 110	9 60
10 40	10 80	10 9	10 3	10 40	10 20

Unit 11 Multiplication: Multiples and common multiples

Set A	Set B	Set C	Set D	Set E	Set F
1 3 times table	1 56	1 35, 84	1 22	1 4	1 35
2 8 times table	2 88	2 10, 24	2 29	2 6	2 12
3 5 times table	3 32	3 45, 108	3 41	3 15	3 8
4 9 times table	4 72	4 55, 132	4 50	4 12	4 4th
5 11 times table	5 40	5 20, 48	5 22	5 10	5 60
6 2 times table	6 96	6 40, 96	6 59	6 20	6 20
7 1 times table	7 80	7 25, 60	7 7	7 8	7 no
8 12 times table	8 48	8 60, 144	8 32	8 10	8 yes
9 4 times table	9 64	9 30, 72	9 85	9 56	9 yes
10 7 times table	10 24	10 15, 36	10 19	10 9	10 40

Unit 12 Division: Factors

Set A	Set B	Set C	Set D	Set E	Set F
1 4	1 1, 5	1 6	1 no	1 6	1 yes
2 3	2 1, 2, 3, 6, 9, 18	2 1	2 no	2 2	2 no
3 6	3 1, 2, 3, 4, 6, 8, 12, 24	3 2	3 yes	3 3	3 yes
4 7	4 1, 2, 11, 22	4 1	4 yes	4 5	4 yes
5 8	5 1, 2, 7, 14	5 1	5 no	5 2	5 no
6 10	6 1, 3, 9	6 8	6 yes	6 3	6 1
7 25	7 1, 2, 4, 8	7 4	7 yes	7 4	7 60
8 9	8 1, 11	8 7	8 no	8 1	8 30
9 16	9 1, 2, 4, 8, 16	9 5	9 no	9 4	9 yes
10 33	10 1, 3, 7, 21	10 12	10 yes	10 10	10 yes

Answers

Unit 13 Doubling

	Set A	Set B	Set C	Set D	Set E	Set F
1	48	54	248	724	34	56
2	82	96	464	902	270	250
3	66	38	662	564	474	494
4	86	70	886	946	666	34
5	44	58	872	362	154	74
6	26	92	498	780	268	344
7	64	30	652	528	902	94
8	42	74	834	388	688	76
9	28	50	476	700	924	944
10	68	90	896	964	656	$12.90

Unit 14 Halving

	Set A	Set B	Set C	Set D	Set E	Set F
1	24	13.5	212	416	111	$124
2	13	27.5	432	447	243	$28
3	43	41.5	113	438	440.5	$13.50
4	22	36	421.5	347	194	17
5	31	24.5	410.5	317	true	46
6	40	49.5	223.5	328	false	15th
7	11	19	312.5	227	false	95
8	34	36.5	140.5	235	60.5	94
9	20	29.5	344.5	146	371.5	17
10	33	11.5	242.5	117	499.5	16th

Unit 15 Place value to 1 million

	Set A	Set B	Set C	Set D	Set E	Set F
1	300	70 000	40 000	10	4	5
2	3000	700	400 000	100	6	4
3	3	70 000	40	10	5	105 000
4	30	7	4	100	3	4
5	3000	70	4000	1000	5	6
6	3000	70 000	400 000	1000	between 7 and 0	1000
7	3000	700	4000	10 000	between 0 and 9	1000
8	30	70	40 000	100	5	$200 000
9	3	700	40	10 000	6	10 000
10	30	7	400	100 000	100	10 000

Unit 16 Rounding off to 10 000

	Set A	Set B	Set C	Set D	Set E	Set F
1	150	3500	15 000	100	1000	50 000
2	350	5500	25 000	200	3000	90 000
3	550	7500	45 000	200	3000	40 000
4	750	9500	65 000	600	6000	40 000
5	950	13 500	85 000	1300	7000	90 000
6	1250	17 500	95 000	2300	8000	30 000
7	1450	20 500	115 000	4800	9000	10 000
8	1850	28 500	135 000	6100	10 000	10 000
9	2250	33 500	175 000	8300	11 000	20 000
10	2950	46 500	195 000	9500	13 000	10 000

Answers

Unit 17 Fractions: Fraction of an amount

	Set A	Set B	Set C	Set D	Set E	Set F
1	3	18	2	3	9	40
2	6	45	4	6	7	3
3	14	63	8	12	yes	two
4	32	81	12	18	6	60
5	50	99	16	30	12	4 million
6	78	270	22	33	no	1/4
7	80	450	40	60	12	12
8	130	720	44	90	33	6
9	270	1800	60	300	yes	$5
10	578	9 000	200	3000	400	90

Unit 18 Fractions: Equivalence and simplest form

	Set A	Set B	Set C	Set D	Set E	Set F
1	$\frac{5}{15}$	$\frac{16}{20}$	$\frac{2}{4}$	2	$\frac{1}{6}$	$\frac{1}{4}$
2	$\frac{6}{12}$	$\frac{12}{18}$	$\frac{3}{4}$	4	$\frac{1}{5}$	5
3	$\frac{9}{45}$	$\frac{6}{10}$	$\frac{2}{4}$	5	$\frac{2}{3}$	$\frac{2}{3}$
4	$\frac{8}{32}$	$\frac{15}{50}$	$\frac{3}{5}$	3	$\frac{4}{5}$	$\frac{6}{7}$
5	$\frac{3}{30}$	$\frac{56}{88}$	$\frac{1}{3}$	12	$\frac{1}{3}$	$\frac{4}{5}$
6	$\frac{2}{14}$	$\frac{6}{27}$	$\frac{5}{7}$	8	$\frac{3}{4}$	$\frac{9}{10}$
7	$\frac{6}{66}$	$\frac{20}{24}$	$\frac{6}{8}$	10	$\frac{2}{3}$	$\frac{3}{7}$
8	$\frac{8}{48}$	$\frac{16}{28}$	$\frac{2}{12}$	5	$\frac{1}{2}$	$\frac{4}{7}$
9	$\frac{12}{96}$	$\frac{35}{40}$	$\frac{7}{8}$	9	$\frac{3}{4}$	$\frac{4}{5}$
10	$\frac{3}{36}$	$\frac{132}{144}$	$\frac{2}{10}$	6	$\frac{7}{8}$	$\frac{1}{5}$

Unit 19 Decimals and their fraction equivalences

	Set A	Set B	Set C	Set D	Set E	Set F
1	$\frac{7}{10}$	0.5	$\frac{1}{2}$	$\frac{7}{10}$	3	8 m
2	$\frac{3}{10}$	0.1	$\frac{11}{100}$	$\frac{7}{10}$	5	5 cm
3	$\frac{4}{5}$	0.25	$\frac{3}{5}$	7	9	90 cm
4	$\frac{2}{5}$	0.2	$\frac{7}{100}$	$\frac{7}{100}$	20	$8\frac{95}{100}$ m
5	$\frac{9}{10}$	0.6	$\frac{1}{50}$	700	23	$8\frac{19}{20}$ m
6	$\frac{1}{2}$	0.75	$\frac{9}{100}$	700	76	2 m
7	$\frac{1}{10}$	0.8	$\frac{27}{100}$	$\frac{7}{10}$	83	5 cm
8	$\frac{3}{5}$	0.4	$\frac{2}{5}$	$\frac{7}{100}$	97	40 cm
9	$\frac{1}{5}$	0.7	$\frac{99}{100}$	7	123	$2\frac{45}{100}$ m
10	$\frac{1}{10}$	0.3	$\frac{33}{100}$	$\frac{7}{10}$	2459	$2\frac{9}{20}$ m

Unit 20 Decimals: Addition and subtraction

	Set A	Set B	Set C	Set D	Set E	Set F
1	0.6	0.4	0.93	0.68	0.76	23.6
2	0.8	0.4	0.71	0.18	0.9	$2.35
3	0.7	0.8	0.71	0.15	0.44	4.4
4	0.9	0.1	0.78	0.48	0.8	1.11
5	0.8	0.2	0.94	0.28	0.48	0.12
6	0.35	0.55	0.95	0.36	0.2	76.7
7	0.78	0.23	0.41	0.42	0.57	2.2
8	0.98	0.53	0.94	0.24	0.66	$7.70
9	0.86	0.21	0.94	0.13	0.23	68.7
10	0.99	0.32	0.63	0.22	0.39	22

Answers

Unit 21 Sequences

	Set A	Set B	Set C	Set D	Set E	Set F
1	+10	–4	36	15	1.2	1
2	x10	halving or dividing by 2	48	G	1	1
3	+50	–8	16	C	2	2
4	x2 or doubling	halving or dividing by 2	56	49	1.6	1
5	+19	–100	J	16	10	$\frac{1}{2}$
6	x5	–11	56	82	0.4	1
7	+1 then 2, 3, 4, etc	dividing by 3	125	4:00	2.5	$1\frac{1}{2}$
8	+99	–1 then –2, –3, –4, etc.	P	Dec	1.7	$1\frac{1}{2}$
9	x3	dividing by 10	67	millions	0.1	$\frac{1}{4}$
10	+2 then 4, 6, 8, etc.	dividing by 4	July	autumn	0.6	2

Unit 22 Number strings

	Set A	Set B	Set C	Set D	Set E	Set F
1	44	2	16	6	19	2
2	16	8	30	3	38	14
3	56	13	70	42	38	11
4	53	1	9	8	37	7
5	60	10	121	4	87	22
6	93	13	0	10	69	60
7	11	4	80	4	14	34
8	57	18	64	12	84	90
9	28	4	132	7	42	30
10	150	14	8	10	68	0

Unit 23 Length and perimeter: Conversions and missing sides

	Set A	Set B	Set C	Set D	Set E	Set F
1	113	1.1	1.6	11	4.8 mm	8.2 mm
2	155	1.85	1.9	14	10 cm	14.4 cm
3	192	1.99	2.2	19	12.4 m	29 m
4	277	2.5	3.7	25	16.8 mm	14.8 mm
5	398	3.01	5.5	33	20.4 m	21 mm
6	407	4.48	11	61	22 cm	11 cm
7	493	5.02	17	73	24.4 m	15 m
8	566	6.67	18.5	84	30 mm	41 m
9	788	7.39	19.5	91	40.4 m	49 m
10	1010	9.9	19.9	99	80.8 cm	101 mm

Unit 24 Area: Concept and application

	Set A	Set B	Set C	Set D	Set E	Set F
1	6 square millimetres	3 m	L = 3 cm, W = 2 cm	square metres	10 square metres	false
2	70 square centimetres	5 m	L = 5 m, W = 2 m	square metres	6 square centimetres	true
3	56 square metres	6 mm	L = 7 mm, W = 2 mm	square centimetres	120 square centimetres	true
4	108 square centimetres	11 m	L = 5 m, W = 3 m	square millimetres	800 square metres	true
5	350 square metres	30 m	L = 7 cm, W = 3 cm	square centimetres	90 square millimetres	false
6	880 square millimetres	12 mm	L = 11 mm, W = 2 mm	square centimetres	2 square metres	false
7	7200 square centimetres	10 cm	L = 13 m, W = 2 m	square centimetres	400 square metres	true
8	4000 square metres	1.5 m	L = 9 cm, W = 3 cm	square metres	400 square centimetres	false
9	600 square centimetres	1.5 m	L = 11 m, W = 3 m	square millimetres	70 square millimetres	false
10	1000 square metres	2.5 m	L = 7 mm, W = 5 mm	square centimetres	1 square metre	false

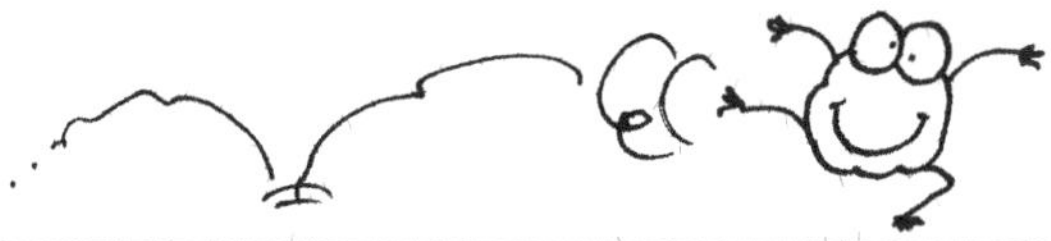

Unit 25 Mass: Units and conversions

	Set A	Set B	Set C	Set D	Set E	Set F
1	500 g	0.1 kg	0.5 kg	3.4 kg	999 g	5
2	900 g	0.4 kg	0.95 kg	2 kg	1 kg	500
3	1000 g	0.8 kg	1 kg	3 kg	1.1 kg	500
4	1100 g	1.2 kg	1 kg	5.5 kg	0.5 kg	2000
5	1500 g	1.3 kg	1.1 kg	8 kg	0.8 kg	2
6	1900 g	1.8 kg	1.5 kg	6 kg	6300 kg	100
7	2200 g	2 kg	2 kg	9.7 kg	7900 kg	10
8	3500 g	2.4 kg	2.7 kg	8 kg	2 t	1.6
9	4500 g	3.1 kg	3.3 kg	9.5 kg	0.1 t	250
10	5700 g	5.5 kg	5.5 kg	10.1 kg	9000 kg	2000

Unit 26 Capacity/volume: Units and conversions

	Set A	Set B	Set C	Set D	Set E	Set F
1	100 mL	0.2 L	8 cubes	1 L	2 cm	1000 cubes
2	500 mL	0.4 L	16 cubes	110 mL	7 cm	27 cubes
3	900 mL	0.8 L	16 cubes	1 L	2 cm	8 cubic centimetres
4	1000 mL	0.95 L	20 cubes	1.1 L	7 m	500 g
5	1100 mL	1 L	24 cubes	0.5 L	6 m	400 L
6	1500 mL	1.2 L	20 cubes	2 L	1 cm	false
7	1900 mL	1.4 L	60 cubes	3000 mL	5 mm	no
8	2200 mL	1.8 L	100 cubes	$\frac{1}{2}$ L	20 cm	64 cubes
9	2500 mL	2 L	120 cubes	$3\frac{1}{2}$ L	100 m	5
10	2900 mL	2.6 L	80 cubes	10 000 mL	5 mm	18

Unit 27 Time: Digital and analogue conversions

	Set A	Set B	Set C	Set D	Set E	Set F
1	17 minutes past 7	8:12	15 minutes	10 minutes	10 hours	11:30
2	25 minutes to 6	3:50	10 minutes	40 minutes	8 hours	3:40 p.m.
3	23 minutes past 10	3:22	30 minutes	70 minutes	7 hours	midnight
4	6 minutes to 2	5:48	60 minutes	120 minutes	6 hours	2:30 a.m.
5	13 minutes to 7	11:15	61 minutes	59 minutes	12 hours	4:48
6	2 minutes to 3	8:45	62 minutes	61 minutes	11 hours	11:04
7	14 minutes past 12	9:56	4 minutes	80 minutes	13 hours	1:55 p.m.
8	26 minutes to 5	7:44	40 minutes	105 minutes	6 hours	9 a.m.
9	11 minutes to 9	1:23	66 minutes	70 minutes	11 hours	afternoon
10	21 minutes past 9	6:49	120 minutes	20 minutes	23 hours	17 minutes

Unit 28 Time: Unit equivalences

	Set A	Set B	Set C	Set D	Set E	Set F
1	$\frac{1}{2}$	$\frac{1}{12}$	Wednesday	November	61 days	9 June
2	$\frac{1}{4}$	$\frac{1}{4}$	Friday	September	61 days	52 Tuesdays
3	$\frac{3}{4}$	$\frac{3}{4}$	Wednesday	March	61 days	July and August
4	$\frac{1}{6}$	$\frac{11}{12}$	Tuesday	March	61 days	December and January
5	$\frac{1}{3}$	$\frac{1}{52}$	Tuesday	May	62 days	5 Fridays
6	$\frac{2}{3}$	$\frac{13}{52}$	Saturday	January	92 days	12 movies
7	$\frac{5}{6}$	$\frac{1}{26}$	Tuesday	March	91 days	20 days
8	$\frac{1}{12}$	$\frac{1}{2}$	Wednesday	December	92 days	21 days
9	$\frac{11}{12}$	$\frac{3}{4}$	Saturday	August	90 days	7 days
10	$\frac{1}{60}$	$\frac{1}{2}$	Sunday	January	91 days	2 fortnights

Answers

Unit 29 Money: Making amounts, addition and subtraction

	Set A	Set B	Set C	Set D	Set E	Set F
1	3 coins	2 notes	4	$1.10	$95.00	$3.85
2	2 coins	3 notes	6	$22.00	$94.15	$185.00
3	3 coins	4 notes	4	$25.00	$92.00	$100 note
4	3 coins	2 notes	8	$45.80	$91.25	$20 note
5	3 coins	4 notes	6	$53.55	$90.25	$100 note
6	3 coins	4 notes	5	$38.65	$80.05	4 coins
7	5 coins	5 notes	9	$94.80	$72.00	3 notes and 2 coins
8	4 coins	7 notes	5	$19.90	$71.10	10 coins
9	7 coins	7 notes	8	$174.00	$53.00	64 coins
10	8 coins	12 notes	11	$330.55	$52.35	no

Unit 30 2D and 3D: Properties and directions

	Set A	Set B	Set C	Set D	Set E	Set F
1	square	6 polygons	south	north and west	$\frac{1}{4}$ turn left	3 rectangles
2	square and triangle	3 polygons	east	south and west	$\frac{1}{2}$ turn either right or left	cone
3	square and rectangle	4 polygons	north	north-east and south-east	$\frac{1}{2}$ turn either right or left	Northern Territory
4	circle and rectangle	6 polygons	west	south-east and south-west	$\frac{1}{4}$ turn left	4 triangles
5	hexagon and triangle	5 polygons	south-east	north and east	$\frac{1}{2}$ turn either right or left	4 faces
6	triangle and rectangle	5 polygons	north-west	north-east and north-west	$\frac{1}{4}$ turn right	west
7	hexagon and rectangle	6 polygons	south-west	south and east	$\frac{1}{4}$ turn right	north-west
8	pentagon and rectangle	7 polygons	north-east	north-west and south-west	$\frac{1}{4}$ turn right	east
9	pentagon and triangle	7 polygons	east	south-west and north-west	$\frac{1}{4}$ turn left	rectangular prism
10	triangle	8 polygons	west	south and west	$\frac{1}{2}$ turn either right or left	sphere

Unit 31 Chance: Concepts of likelihood

	Set A	Set B	Set C	Set D	Set E	Set F
1	15 cards	unlikely	an odd card	$\frac{1}{30}$	true	4 cards
2	15 cards	50/50	an odd card	$\frac{1}{10}$	false	$\frac{2}{15}$
3	10 cards	likely	50/50	$\frac{1}{2}$	false	26 cards
4	18 cards	unlikely	50/50	$\frac{1}{2}$	false	$\frac{13}{15}$
5	24 cards	likely	50/50	$\frac{1}{3}$	true	6 cards
6	16 cards	unlikely	50/50	$\frac{1}{3}$	false	$\frac{1}{5}$
7	5 cards	impossible	50/50	$\frac{2}{3}$	true	10 cards
8	0 cards	certain	a card bigger than 15	$\frac{1}{6}$	true	$\frac{1}{3}$
9	5 cards	likely	50/50	$\frac{1}{6}$	true	5 cards
10	5 cards	unlikely	a blue 22 card	$\frac{2}{3}$	false	$\frac{1}{6}$

Unit 32 Revision: All sorts

	Set A	Set B	Set C	Set D	Set E	Set F
1	63	1500	–8	197	12	14 m
2	58	6	5	97	2 factors	false
3	46	52	70 cm	106	48	4 kg
4	42	41.5	7500 g	32	15	1000 cubic centimetres
5	54	6 million	8000 mL	21	99 999	60 days
6	108	23 500	24 minutes to 5	72	78 000	9 hours
7	9	9	winter	12 000	0.25	$1.45
8	11	$\frac{1}{4}$	1600 square millimetres	11	0.6	triangles
9	20	0.13	13 five cents	12	64	rectangles
10	70	0.72	rectangular prism	60	50	50/50

Set C

What is the 4 worth in the following numbers?

1 **243 659** ________

2 **462 880** ________

3 **263 749** ________

4 **213 664** ________

5 **804 779** ________

6 **432 816** ________

7 **384 565** ________

8 **340 008** ________

9 **221 849** ________

10 **892 455** ________

Set D

How many times bigger is the first 5 than the second 5 in the following numbers?

1 **355** ________

2 **515** ________

3 **5569** ________

4 **2595** ________

5 **5785** ________

6 **25 435** ________

7 **58 305** ________

8 **515 233** ________

9 **657 985** ________

10 **590 005** ________

Set F

1 The MCG holds ninety thousand people. How many digits in this number? ____

2 How many zeros are in the number ninety thousand? ____

3 Eden Gardens Calcutta holds one hundred and five thousand people. Write this number down. __________

4 How many zeros are in the number one hundred and five thousand? ____

5 How many digits are in the number one hundred and five thousand? ____

6 At $10 a ticket, how many tickets need to be sold to take $10 000? _______

7 At $100 a ticket, how many need to be sold to take $100 000? _______

8 A band earns $10 for each CD they sell. 20 000 sales gives them $ __________.

9 How many metres does an athlete cover in the 10 km walk? _______

10 How many decades equal 100 000 years? _______

Number and Algebra

Unit 16 Rounding off to 10 000

When numbers are rounded off, they are taken to the nearest 10, 100, 1000 or 10 000. If a number is exactly halfway, it is taken up, not down. So, 250 to the nearest 100 would equal 300; 55 000 to the nearest 10 000 would be 60 000, and so on.

Set A

Find the number that is halfway between:

1 100 and 200 ______

2 300 and 400 ______

3 500 and 600 ______

4 700 and 800 ______

5 900 and 1000 ______

6 1200 and 1300 ______

7 1400 and 1500 ______

8 1800 and 1900 ______

9 2200 and 2300 ______

10 2900 and 3000 ______

Set B

Find the number that is halfway between:

1 3000 and 4000 ______

2 5000 and 6000 ______

3 7000 and 8000 ______

4 9000 and 10 000 ______

5 13 000 and 14 000 ______

6 17 000 and 18 000 ______

7 20 000 and 21 000 ______

8 28 000 and 29 000 ______

9 33 000 and 34 000 ______

10 46 000 and 47 000 ______

Set E

Round these numbers to the nearest 1000.

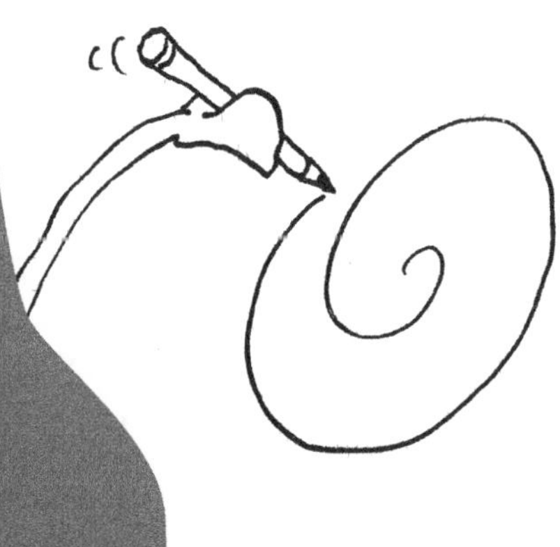

1 1351 ______

2 2509 ______

3 3400 ______

4 6050 ______

5 6500 ______

6 8348 ______

7 9494 ______

8 10 199 ______

9 10 500 ______

10 12 611 ______

Set C

Find the number that is halfway between:

1 **10 000 and 20 000** ________

2 **20 000 and 30 000** ________

3 **40 000 and 50 000** ________

4 **60 000 and 70 000** ________

5 **80 000 and 90 000** ________

6 **90 000 and 100 000** ________

7 **110 000 and 120 000** ________

8 **130 000 and 140 000** ________

9 **170 000 and 180 000** ________

10 **190 000 and 200 000** ________

Set D

Round these numbers to the nearest 100.

1 **145** [ ]

2 **151** [ ]

3 **249** [ ]

4 **560** [ ]

5 **1288** [ ]

6 **2335** [ ]

7 **4759** [ ]

8 **6109** [ ]

9 **8328** [ ]

10 **9549** [ ]

Set F

Round these numbers to the nearest 10 000.

1 The SCG crowd: 52 898 ________

2 The Telstra Stadium crowd: 87 611 ________

3 The Gabba crowd: 44 972 ________

4 The AAMI Stadium crowd: 37 235 ________

5 The MCG crowd: 93 667 ________

6 The Subiaco Oval crowd: 25 773 ________

7 The Bundaberg Rum Stadium crowd: 11 732 ________

8 The Marrara Oval crowd: 8562 ________

9 The Manuka Oval crowd: 17 834 ________

10 The York Park Oval crowd: 14 401 ________

Number and Algebra

Unit 17

Fractions: Fraction of an amount

Remember that when we deal with fractions, we are really just working with division. Finding half of an amount means dividing it into two equal parts and taking one of those parts. Finding two-thirds of an amount means splitting it into three equal parts and taking two of those parts.

Set A

Find one-tenth of:

1	30	
2	60	
3	140	
4	320	
5	500	
6	780	
7	800	
8	1300	
9	2700	
10	5780	

Set B

Find nine-tenths of:

1	20	
2	50	
3	70	
4	90	
5	110	
6	300	
7	500	
8	800	
9	2000	
10	10 000	

Set E

1 What is one-third of 27? ____

2 Find one-sixth of 42 ____

3 Is two-fifths of 10 equal to 4? ____

4 What is two-sevenths of 21? ____

5 Find three-tenths of 40 ____

6 Is nine-tenths of 80 equal to 70? ____

7 Find six-twelfths of 24 ____

8 Find four-eighths of 66 ____

9 Is three-sixths of 100 the same as one-half of 100? ____

10 What is four-fifths of 500? ____

Set C

Find two-thirds of:

1	3	
2	6	
3	12	
4	18	
5	24	
6	33	
7	60	
8	66	
9	90	
10	300	

Set D

Find three-quarters of:

1	4	
2	8	
3	16	
4	24	
5	40	
6	44	
7	80	
8	120	
9	400	
10	4000	

Set F

1 One-third of the 60 apples were bad and had to be thrown out. ____ apples were kept.

2 At the party, nine-tenths of the 30 cola cans were drunk. ____ cans remained.

3 Five-sevenths of the world's surface is water; ____ -sevenths is land.

4 Six-sevenths of an iceberg is under water. If 10 metres shows, ____ metres are under water.

5 About one-fifth of Australia's 20 million people live in Melbourne. About ____________ people are Melburnians.

6 I ate 250 grams of the kilo of grapes we bought. I ate what fraction of a kilo? ____

7 We won three-quarters of the 16 games we played this season. We won ____ games.

8 It rained for one-fifth of the days in November. It rained for ____ days.

9 I spent one-ninth of my $45 on a book. The book cost $ ____.

10 Samantha led for nine-tenths of the 100 m race. She led the race for ____ metres.

Unit 18 Fractions: Equivalence and simplest form

Number and Algebra

Remember that equal or equivalent fractions are fractions that are the same size but are expressed using different numerals, for example $\frac{1}{2}$ and $\frac{5}{10}$.

Fractions are in their simplest form when the numbers used to show their size are the smallest possible, for example $\frac{1}{2}$ rather than $\frac{5}{10}$.

Set A

Form equal fractions.

1. $\frac{1}{3} = \frac{\ }{15}$
2. $\frac{1}{2} = \frac{\ }{12}$
3. $\frac{1}{5} = \frac{\ }{45}$
4. $\frac{1}{4} = \frac{\ }{32}$
5. $\frac{1}{10} = \frac{\ }{30}$
6. $\frac{1}{7} = \frac{\ }{14}$
7. $\frac{1}{11} = \frac{\ }{66}$
8. $\frac{1}{6} = \frac{\ }{48}$
9. $\frac{1}{8} = \frac{\ }{96}$
10. $\frac{1}{12} = \frac{\ }{36}$

Set B

Form equal fractions.

1. $\frac{4}{5} = \frac{\ }{20}$
2. $\frac{2}{3} = \frac{\ }{18}$
3. $\frac{3}{5} = \frac{\ }{10}$
4. $\frac{3}{10} = \frac{\ }{50}$
5. $\frac{7}{11} = \frac{\ }{88}$
6. $\frac{2}{9} = \frac{\ }{27}$
7. $\frac{5}{6} = \frac{\ }{24}$
8. $\frac{4}{7} = \frac{\ }{28}$
9. $\frac{7}{8} = \frac{\ }{40}$
10. $\frac{11}{12} = \frac{\ }{144}$

Set E

Put the following fractions into their simplest forms.

1. $\frac{3}{18}$ ____
2. $\frac{5}{25}$ ____
3. $\frac{8}{12}$ ____
4. $\frac{12}{15}$ ____
5. $\frac{20}{60}$ ____
6. $\frac{18}{24}$ ____
7. $\frac{14}{21}$ ____
8. $\frac{15}{30}$ ____
9. $\frac{27}{36}$ ____
10. $\frac{14}{16}$ ____

Set C

Form equal fractions.

1 $\frac{4}{8} = \frac{\_}{4}$

2 $\frac{15}{20} = \frac{\_}{4}$

3 $\frac{8}{16} = \frac{\_}{4}$

4 $\frac{15}{25} = \frac{\_}{5}$

5 $\frac{10}{30} = \frac{\_}{3}$

6 $\frac{25}{35} = \frac{5}{\_}$

7 $\frac{36}{48} = \frac{6}{\_}$

8 $\frac{20}{120} = \frac{2}{\_}$

9 $\frac{42}{48} = \frac{7}{\_}$

10 $\frac{20}{100} = \frac{2}{\_}$

Set D

Simplify the following fractions by changing them into whole numbers.

1 $\frac{8}{4} =$ ☐

2 $\frac{12}{3} =$ ☐

3 $\frac{25}{5} =$ ☐

4 $\frac{24}{8} =$ ☐

5 $\frac{36}{3} =$ ☐

6 $\frac{80}{10} =$ ☐

7 $\frac{70}{7} =$ ☐

8 $\frac{45}{9} =$ ☐

9 $\frac{63}{7} =$ ☐

10 $\frac{66}{11} =$ ☐

Set F

1 A pizza was cut into 8 slices and I ate 2 slices. I ate ____ of the pizza.

2 I played 20 quarters of football this year, or ____ games of football.

3 4 of my 6 cards were black; ____ of the cards were black.

4 I placed 12 of my 14 serves correctly. ____ of my serves were good.

5 8 of my 10 notes were $10 notes. ____ were $10 notes.

6 I played 90 of the 100 notes on my flute correctly. ____ of the notes were correct.

7 6 of our 14 pets are carnivores. ____ are carnivores.

8 ____ of our pets are not carnivores.

9 8 of the 10 candles on the cake were blown out. ____ were blown out.

10 ____ of the candles stayed alight.

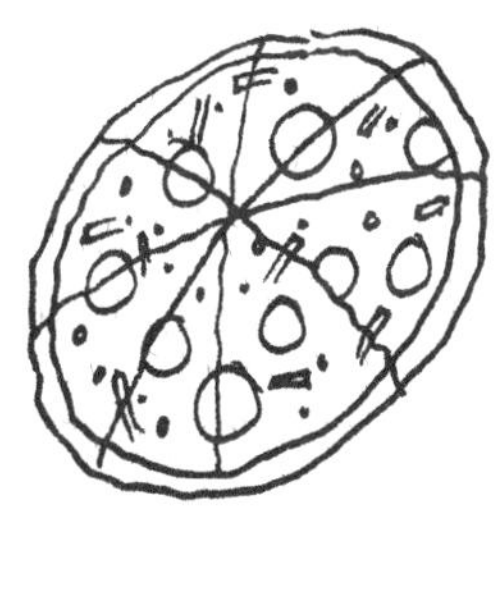

Number and Algebra

Unit 19
Decimals and their fraction equivalences

Remember that the first decimal place following the decimal point deals with tenths and that the second decimal place deals with hundredths. So 3.17 can be written as $3\frac{17}{100}$.

Set A

Change these decimals to fractions in simplest form.

1 0.7 ☐
2 0.3 ☐
3 0.8 ☐
4 0.4 ☐
5 0.9 ☐
6 0.5 ☐
7 0.1 ☐
8 0.6 ☐
9 0.2 ☐
10 0.10 ☐

Set B

Change these fractions into decimals.

1 $\frac{1}{2}$ ☐
2 $\frac{1}{10}$ ☐
3 $\frac{1}{4}$ ☐
4 $\frac{1}{5}$ ☐
5 $\frac{3}{5}$ ☐
6 $\frac{3}{4}$ ☐
7 $\frac{4}{5}$ ☐
8 $\frac{2}{5}$ ☐
9 $\frac{7}{10}$ ☐
10 $\frac{3}{10}$ ☐

Set E

Round each of these decimals to the nearest whole number.

1 3.47 _____
2 4.51 _____
3 8.50 _____
4 19.64 _____
5 23.07 _____
6 76.49 _____
7 82.83 _____
8 97.08 _____
9 123.09 _____
10 2458.52 _____

Set C

Change these decimals into fractions in simplest form.

1 0.50 ______
2 0.11 ______
3 0.60 ______
4 0.07 ______
5 0.02 ______
6 0.09 ______
7 0.27 ______
8 0.40 ______
9 0.99 ______
10 0.33 ______

Set D

What is the 7 worth in the following decimals?

1 5.79 ______
2 12.76 ______
3 7.11 ______
4 89.97 ______
5 789.32 ______
6 2734.09 ______
7 2348.73 ______
8 3486.97 ______
9 2857.92 ______
10 2 332 245.75 ______

Set F

1 8.95 metres is the world long-jump record. What is the value of the 8? ________
2 What is the value of the 5? ________
3 What is the value of the 9? ________
4 Change this length to a whole number and a fraction. ________
5 Now write this length as a whole number and a fraction in simplest form. ________
6 The world high-jump record is 2.45 metres. What is the value of the 2? ________
7 What is the value of the 5? ________
8 What is the value of the 4? ________
9 Change this height into a whole number and a fraction. ________
10 Now write the height as a whole number and a fraction in simplest form. ________

Number and Algebra

Unit 20
Decimals: Addition and subtraction

Adding and subtracting with decimals is no harder than with whole numbers. Just ensure that all the numerals you are dealing with have an equal number of decimal places. For example, change 0.7 + 0.03 to 0.70 + 0.03 to avoid confusion.

Set A

1 0.4 + 0.2 = ☐

2 0.3 + 0.5 = ☐

3 0.5 + 0.2 = ☐

4 0.2 + 0.7 = ☐

5 0.5 + 0.3 = ☐

6 0.12 + 0.23 = ☐

7 0.33 + 0.45 = ☐

8 0.22 + 0.76 = ☐

9 0.13 + 0.73 = ☐

10 0.45 + 0.54 = ☐

Set B

1 0.8 – 0.4 = ☐

2 0.6 – 0.2 = ☐

3 0.9 – 0.1 = ☐

4 0.7 – 0.6 = ☐

5 0.4 – 0.2 = ☐

6 0.87 – 0.32 = ☐

7 0.58 – 0.35 = ☐

8 0.99 – 0.46 = ☐

9 0.55 – 0.34 = ☐

10 0.72 – 0.40 = ☐

Set E

1 Find the sum of 0.2 and 0.56 _____

2 Add 0.5 to 0.4 _____

3 What is 0.1 and 0.34 altogether? _____

4 What is the total of 0.2, 0.2 and 0.4? _____

5 Combine 0.11 and 0.37 _____

6 Find the difference between 0.6 and 0.4 _____

7 Reduce 0.79 by 0.22 _____

8 Take 0.3 away from 0.96 _____

9 Subtract 0.7 from 0.93 _____

10 Remove 0.11 from 0.5 _____

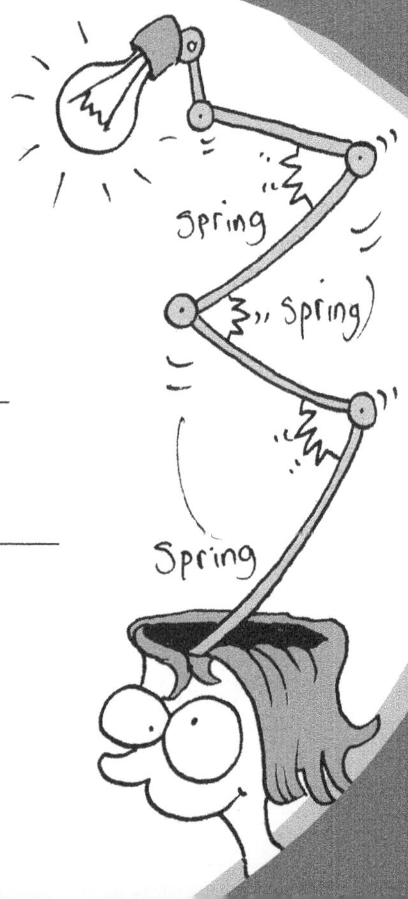

Set C

1 $0.7 + 0.23 =$ ☐

2 $0.41 + 0.3 =$ ☐

3 $0.6 + 0.11 =$ ☐

4 $0.48 + 0.3 =$ ☐

5 $0.8 + 0.14 =$ ☐

6 $0.35 + 0.6 =$ ☐

7 $0.2 + 0.21 =$ ☐

8 $0.44 + 0.5 =$ ☐

9 $0.1 + 0.3 + 0.54 =$ ☐

10 $0.11 + 0.22 + 0.3 =$ ☐

Set D

1 $0.8 - 0.12 =$ ☐

2 $0.78 - 0.6 =$ ☐

3 $0.3 - 0.15 =$ ☐

4 $0.88 - 0.4 =$ ☐

5 $0.4 - 0.12 =$ ☐

6 $0.66 - 0.3 =$ ☐

7 $0.7 - 0.28 =$ ☐

8 $0.4 - 0.16 =$ ☐

9 $0.23 - 0.1 =$ ☐

10 $0.9 - 0.68 =$ ☐

Set F

1 The temperature was 34.6 degrees and then fell 11 degrees to _____ degrees.

2 I had $4.55 but lost $2.20. I then only had $_____ left to spend.

3 The school long-jump record of 4.25 m was beaten by 0.15 m. The new record is _____ m.

4 A strike run rate of 4.46 was needed, but we scored at 3.35. Our rate was _____ short.

5 Our tallest teacher is 2.02 m. A doorjamb is 2.14 m. The difference is _____ m.

6 Dad weighs 76.5 kg and ate an apple weighing 0.2 kg. Dad now weighs _____ kg.

7 The cross-country race is 4.5 km and I have run 2.3 km. _____ km to go!

8 $7.7 is more commonly written as $ _____.

9 I swam two laps in 33.5 sec and 35.2 sec, a total time of _____ sec.

10 I live 2.2 km from school. In a week of going to and from school I travel _____ km.

Number and Algebra

Unit 21 Sequences

A sequence is a pattern including numbers, letters or symbols. Each member of a sequence is called a term and each sequence's pattern is called a rule. The sequence 3, 6, 9, . . . has 6 as its second term and the rule of +3 or the 3 times table.

Set A

What is the rule for each of the following sequences?

1 **3, 13, 23, 33, . . .** ______

2 **3, 30, 300, . . .** ______

3 **12, 62, 112, 162, . . .** ______

4 **3, 6, 12, 24, . . .** ______

5 **15, 34, 53, 72, . . .** ______

6 **1, 5, 25, 125, . . .** ______

7 **1, 2, 4, 7, 11, . . .** ______

8 **6, 105, 204, 303, . . .** ______

9 **2, 6 ,18, 54, . . .** ______

10 **1, 3, 7, 13, 21, . . .** ______

Set B

What is the rule for each of the following sequences?

1 **27, 23, 19, 15, . . .** ______

2 **120, 60, 30, 15, . . .** ______

3 **65, 57, 49, 41, . . .** ______

4 **64, 32, 16, 8, . . .** ______

5 **787, 687, 587, . . .** ______

6 **132, 121, 110, 99, . . .** ______

7 **81, 27, 9, 3, . . .** ______

8 **43, 42, 40, 37, 33, . . .** ______

9 **1200, 120, 12, 1.2, . . .** ______

10 **64, 16, 4, 1, . . .** ______

Set C

Find the missing term.

1 18, 27, ____ , 45

2 36, ____ , 60, 72

3 4, 8, ____ , 32

4 7, 14, 28, ____ , 112

5 A, D, G, ____

6 63, ____ , 49, 42

7 500, 250, ____ , 62.5

8 Z, Y, W, T, ____

9 100, 89, 78, ____ , 56

10 Jan, Mar, May, ____

Set D

Find the 7th term for each of the following sequences.

1 3, 5, 7, 9, . . . ____

2 A, B, C, . . . ____

3 W, X, Y, Z, . . . ____

4 7, 14, 21, 28, . . . ____

5 $\frac{1}{4}$, $\frac{1}{2}$, 1, 2, . . . ____

6 100, 97, 94, 91, . . . ____

7 1:00, 1:30, 2:00, 2:30, . . . ____

8 Dec, Oct, Aug, Jun, . . . ____

9 ones, tens, hundreds, thousands, . . . ____

10 spring, summer, autumn, . . . ____

Set E

Find the missing term.

1 0.6, 0.8, 1, ____

2 0.1, 0.4, 0.7, ____

3 0.5, 1, 1.5, ____

4 0.2, 0.4, 0.8, ____

5 0.01, 0.1, 1, ____

6 1.6, 1.2, 0.8, ____

7 20, 10, 5, ____

8 3.8, 3.1, 2.4, ____

9 100, 10, 1, ____

10 2.1, 1.6, 1.2, 0.9, 0.7, ____

Set F

Find the missing term.

1 $\frac{1}{3}$, $\frac{2}{3}$, ____, $1\frac{1}{3}$

2 $\frac{1}{5}$, $\frac{3}{5}$, ____, $1\frac{2}{5}$

3 $\frac{1}{4}$, $\frac{1}{2}$, 1, ____

4 $\frac{1}{10}$, $\frac{4}{10}$, $\frac{7}{10}$, ____

5 $\frac{1}{8}$, $\frac{1}{4}$, $\frac{3}{8}$, ____

6 $\frac{1}{4}$, $\frac{1}{2}$, $\frac{3}{4}$, ____

7 6, $4\frac{1}{2}$, 3, ____

8 12, 6, 3, ____

9 2, 1, $\frac{1}{2}$, ____

10 8, $6\frac{1}{2}$, 5, $3\frac{1}{2}$, ____

Number and Algebra

Unit 22 Number strings

Number strings are questions made up of many smaller pieces. Work left to right to solve these challenging problems. However, remember that anything in a bracket must be done first.

Set A

1 5 x 8 + 4 = ☐

2 6 x 3 – 2 = ☐

3 12 x 4 + 8 = ☐

4 7 x 8 – 3 = ☐

5 5 x 11 + 5 = ☐

6 9 x 9 + 12 = ☐

7 8 x 2 – 5 = ☐

8 6 x 9 + 3 = ☐

9 3 x 11 – 5 = ☐

10 12 x 12 + 6 = ☐

Set B

1 25 ÷ 5 – 3 = ☐

2 36 ÷ 6 + 2 = ☐

3 100 ÷ 10 + 3 = ☐

4 24 ÷ 4 – 5 = ☐

5 44 ÷ 11 + 6 = ☐

6 30 ÷ 5 + 7 = ☐

7 84 ÷ 12 – 3 = ☐

8 63 ÷ 7 + 9 = ☐

9 144 ÷ 12 – 8 = ☐

10 42 ÷ 6 + 7 = ☐

Set E

1 5 x 3 + 8 – 4 = ☐

2 7 x 5 + 10 – 7 = ☐

3 12 x 3 - 7 + 9 = ☐

4 5 x 8 + 4 – 7 = ☐

5 12 x 7 – 3 + 6 = ☐

6 8 x 8 + 10 – 5 = ☐

7 8 x 3 – 3 – 7 = ☐

8 11 x 7 + 4 + 3 = ☐

9 9 x 4 – 6 + 12 = ☐

10 8 x 8 + 12 – 8 = ☐

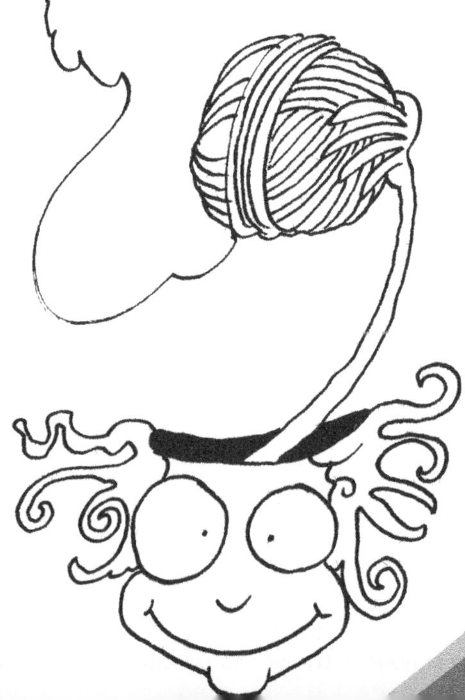

Set C

1 2 x (5 + 3) = ☐

2 5 x (12 – 6) = ☐

3 7 x (8 + 2) = ☐

4 3 x (7 – 4) = ☐

5 11 x (2 + 9) = ☐

6 6 x (4 – 4) = ☐

7 10 x (2 + 6) = ☐

8 8 x (12 – 4) = ☐

9 12 x (7 + 4) = ☐

10 2 x (11 – 7) = ☐

Set D

1 12 ÷ (10 – 8) = ☐

2 15 ÷ (3 + 2) = ☐

3 42 ÷ (6 – 5) = ☐

4 64 ÷ (3 + 5) = ☐

5 32 ÷ (14 – 6) = ☐

6 90 ÷ (14 – 5) = ☐

7 36 ÷ (4 + 5) = ☐

8 120 ÷ (14 – 4) = ☐

9 49 ÷ (16 – 9) = ☐

10 70 ÷ (14 – 7) = ☐

Set F

1 30 ÷ 6 – 5 + 2 = ☐

2 25 ÷ 5 + 6 + 3 = ☐

3 54 ÷ 9 – 6 + 11 = ☐

4 110 ÷ 10 + 4 – 8 = ☐

5 16 ÷ 8 + 12 + 8 = ☐

6 50 ÷ 5 x 7 – 8 – 2 = ☐

7 88 ÷ 11 x 4 – 4 + 6 = ☐

8 32 ÷ 4 x 10 + 12 – 2 = ☐

9 14 ÷ 2 x 3 + 7 + 2 = ☐

10 72 ÷ 6 x 5 ÷ 12 – 5 = ☐

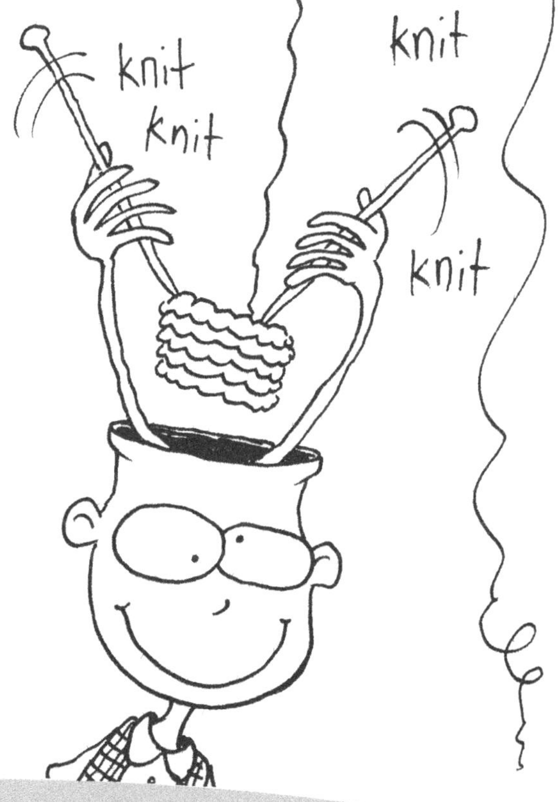

Measurement and Geometry

Unit 23 Length and Perimeter: Conversions and missing sides

Remember that, in measurement,
10 mm = 1 cm
100 cm = 1 m
1000 m = 1 km.
Therefore,
1 mm = 0.1 cm
1 cm = 0.01 m
1 m = 0.001 km.

Set A

1 1.13 m = ______ cm
2 1.55 m = ______ cm
3 1.92 m = ______ cm
4 2.77 m = ______ cm
5 3.98 m = ______ cm
6 4.07 m = ______ cm
7 4.93 m = ______ cm
8 5.66 m = ______ cm
9 7.88 m = ______ cm
10 10.1 m = ______ cm

Set B

1 110 cm = ______ m
2 185 cm = ______ m
3 199 cm = ______ m
4 250 cm = ______ m
5 301 cm = ______ m
6 448 cm = ______ m
7 502 cm = ______ m
8 667 cm = ______ m
9 739 cm = ______ m
10 990 cm = ______ m

Set E

What would the perimeter of a square be with side lengths of:

1 1.2 mm? ________
2 2.5 cm? ________
3 3.1 m? ________
4 4.2 mm? ________
5 5.1 m? ________
6 5.5 cm? ________
7 6.1 m? ________
8 7.5 mm? ________
9 10.1 m? ________
10 20.2 cm? ________

Set C

1 16 mm = ______ cm

2 19 mm = ______ cm

3 22 mm = ______ cm

4 37 mm = ______ cm

5 55 mm = ______ cm

6 110 mm = ______ cm

7 170 mm = ______ cm

8 185 mm = ______ cm

9 195 mm = ______ cm

10 199 mm = ______ cm

Set D

1 1.1 cm = _____ mm

2 1.4 cm = _____ mm

3 1.9 cm = _____ mm

4 2.5 cm = _____ mm

5 3.3 cm = _____ mm

6 6.1 cm = _____ mm

7 7.3 cm = _____ mm

8 8.4 cm = _____ mm

9 9.1 cm = _____ mm

10 9.9 cm = _____ mm

Set F

What would the perimeter of a rectangle be if its side lengths were:

1 L = 3 mm, W = 1.1 mm? _________

2 L = 5 cm, W = 2.2 cm? _________

3 L = 10 m, W = 4.5 m? _________

4 L = 6 mm, W = 1.4 mm? _________

5 L = 7 mm, W = 3.5 mm? _________

6 L = 4 cm, W = 1.5 cm? _________

7 L = 5 m, W = 2.5 m? _________

8 L = 11 m, W = 9.5 m? _________

9 L = 20 m, W = 4.5 m? _________

10 L = 50 mm, W = 0.5 mm? _________

Measurement and Geometry

Unit 24
Area: Concept and application

Area deals with the space inside a boundary or perimeter. Remember that the area of a rectangle is worked out by multiplying together the length and the width. This divides the shape into squares such as square centimetres or square metres.

Set A

What would the areas of the following rectangles be?

1 L = 3 mm, W = 2 mm, A = ________

2 L = 10 cm, W = 7 cm, A = ________

3 L = 8 m, W = 7 m, A = ________

4 L = 12 cm, W = 9 cm, A = ________

5 L = 70 m, W = 5 m, A = ________

6 L = 110 mm, W = 8 mm, A = ________

7 L = 90 cm, W = 80 cm, A = ________

8 L = 100 m, W = 40 m, A = ________

9 L = 200 cm, W = 3 cm, A = ________

10 L = 100 m, W = 10 m, A = ________

Set B

Find the widths of the following rectangles.

1 L = 12 m, A = 36 sq m, W = _____

2 L = 8 m, A = 40 sq m, W = _____

3 L = 7 mm, A = 42 sq mm, W = _____

4 L = 90 m, A = 990 sq m, W = _____

5 L = 60 m, A = 1800 sq m, W = _____

6 L = 30 mm, A = 360 sq mm, W = _____

7 L = 100 cm, A = 1000 sq cm, W = _____

8 L = 2 m, A = 3 sq m, W = _____

9 L = 6 m, A = 9 sq m, W = _____

10 L = 10 m, A = 25 sq m, W = _____

Set E

Circle the most sensible measure for the area of:

1 a garden bed. 10 square: millimetres, centimetres or metres?

2 a stamp. 6 square: millimetres, centimetres or metres?

3 an envelope. 120 square: millimetres, centimetres or metres?

4 a soccer pitch. 800 square: millimetres, centimetres or metres?

5 a small sticker. 90 square: millimetres, centimetres or metres?

6 a tabletop. 2 square: millimetres, centimetres or metres?

7 a basketball court. 400 square: millimetres, centimetres or metres?

8 a tissue. 400 square: millimetres, centimetres or metres?

9 a calculator button. 70 square: millimetres, centimetres or metres?

10 a fly screen.1 square: millimetre, centimetre or metre?

Set C

What must the length and the width of the following rectangles be, given these areas? (Note: The lengths and widths are whole numbers bigger than 1.)

1 **6 sq cm: L = _____, W = _____**

2 **10 sq m: L = _____, W = _____**

3 **14 sq mm: L = _____, W = _____**

4 **15 sq m: L = _____, W = _____**

5 **21 sq cm: L = _____, W = _____**

6 **22 sq mm: L = _____, W = _____**

7 **26 sq m: L = _____, W = _____**

8 **27 sq cm: L = _____, W = _____**

9 **33 sq m: L = _____, W = _____**

10 **35 sq mm: L = _____, W = _____**

Set D

Would you use square centimetres, square millimetres or square metres to measure the area of:

1 **a kitchen?** __________________

2 **a garden bed?** __________________

3 **the front cover of a CD?** __________________

4 **a pin head?** __________________

5 **a piece of A3 paper?** __________________

6 **an atlas map of Australia?** __________________

7 **a computer screen?** __________________

8 **a roof?** __________________

9 **a baby's little fingernail?** __________________

10 **a napkin?** __________________

Set F

Answer 'true' or 'false' to the following statements.

1 Queensland has the largest area of all Australia's states. ________

2 Tasmania is Australia's smallest state in area. ________

3 The area of a square is calculated by length x width. ________

4 The area of a rectangle is calculated by length x width. ________

5 The area of a house should be calculated in square centimetres. ________

6 The perimeter of a room could be 28 square metres. ________

7 House painters deal with area in their work. ________

8 Lines around a hockey field are examples of area. ________

9 Roof tiles are sold by the square centimetre. ________

10 10 centimetres x 10 centimetres = 1 square metre. ________

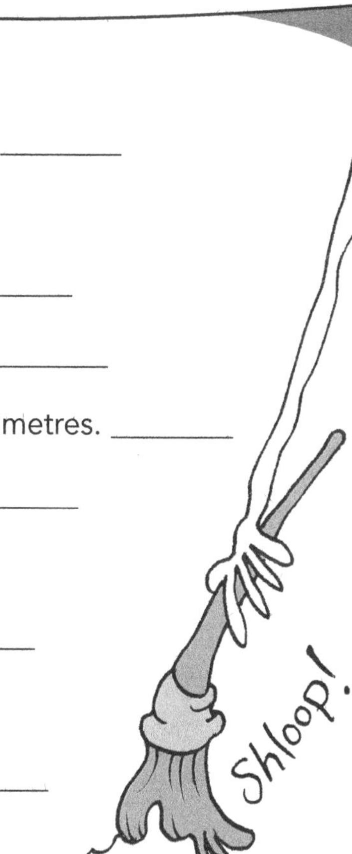

Measurement and Geometry

Unit 25
Mass: Units and conversions

Remember that 1000 grams equals 1 kilogram and that 1000 kilograms equals 1 tonne.

The abbreviations for these measures are g, kg and t.

Remember also that 1 litre of water weighs 1 kilogram.

Set A

Convert the following masses into grams.

1 **0.5 kg** ________
2 **0.9 kg** ________
3 **1.0 kg** ________
4 **1.1 kg** ________
5 **1.5 kg** ________
6 **1.9 kg** ________
7 **2.2 kg** ________
8 **3.5 kg** ________
9 **4.5 kg** ________
10 **5.7 kg** ________

Set B

Change these masses into kilograms.

1 **100 g** ________
2 **400 g** ________
3 **800 g** ________
4 **1200 g** ________
5 **1300 g** ________
6 **1800 g** ________
7 **2000 g** ________
8 **2400 g** ________
9 **3100 g** ________
10 **5500 g** ________

Set E

Circle the greater mass.

1 999 g or 0.1 kg ________
2 1 kg or 100 g ________
3 1000 g or 1.1 kg ________
4 0.5 kg or 60 g ________
5 700 g or 0.8 kg ________
6 6300 kg or 1 t ________
7 7900 kg or 1 t ________
8 2 t or 300 kg ________
9 0.1 kg or 0.1 t ________
10 9000 kg or 1 t ________

Set C

How much would the following quantities of water weigh?

1 500 mL ______
2 950 mL ______
3 1000 mL ______
4 1 L ______
5 1.1 L ______
6 1.5 L ______
7 2 L ______
8 2.7 L ______
9 3.3 L ______
10 5.5 L ______

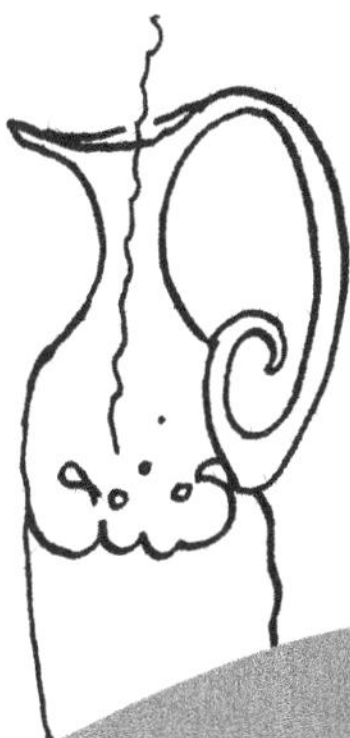

Set D

Combine the following masses.

1 1.2 kg and 2.2 kg ______
2 1.5 kg and 0.5 kg ______
3 1.8 kg and 1.2 kg ______
4 2.3 kg and 3.2 kg ______
5 3.5 kg and 4.5 kg ______
6 5.1 kg and 0.9 kg ______
7 6.4 kg and 3.3 kg ______
8 7.3 kg and 0.7 kg ______
9 8.3 kg and 1.2 kg ______
10 9 kg and 1.1 kg ______

Set F

1 I filled a 10 litre bucket with water halfway to the top. It weighed ______ kg.
2 My 500 mL glass of water weighs ______ g.
3 A farmer spread half a tonne of fertiliser weighing ______ kg.
4 My spa holds 2000 L of water weighing ______ kg.
5 My spa's water weighs ______ t.
6 If a $1 coin weighs 10 g, ______ coins would weigh 1 kg.
7 I would need ______ glue sticks, each weighing 100 g, to equal 1 kg.
8 My dad's car weighs 1600 kg or ______ t.
9 My novel weighs a quarter of a kilogram or ______ grams.
10 To drop from 68 kg to 66 kg you must lose ______ grams.

Measurement and Geometry

Unit 26
Capacity/volume: Units and conversions

Remember that 1000 millilitres (mL) equals 1 litre (L).

Volume refers to the space inside a 3D object and for cubes and rectangular prisms is calculated by multiplying the number of units in the length by the units in the depth and the units in the height of the object.

Set A

Convert the following capacities into millilitres.

1 **0.1 L** ________
2 **0.5 L** ________
3 **0.9 L** ________
4 **1 L** ________
5 **1.1 L** ________
6 **1.5 L** ________
7 **1.9 L** ________
8 **2.2 L** ________
9 **2.5 L** ________
10 **2.9 L** ________

Set B

Convert the following capacities into litres.

1 **200 mL** ______
2 **400 mL** ______
3 **800 mL** ______
4 **950 mL** ______
5 **1000 mL** ______
6 **1200 mL** ______
7 **1400 mL** ______
8 **1800 mL** ______
9 **2000 mL** ______
10 **2600 mL** ______

Set E

Find the missing side for each of the following volumes of rectangular prisms.

1 L = 5 cm, D = 3 cm, H = _____ cm, V = 30 cubes
2 L = 8 cm, D = _____ cm, H = 1 cm, V = 56 cubes
3 L = 4 cm, D = 3 cm, H = _____ cm, V = 24 cubes
4 L = _____ m, D = 6 m, H = 2 m, V = 84 cubes
5 L =10 m, D = _____ m, H = 2 m, V = 120 cubes
6 L = 10 cm, D = 10 cm, H = _____ cm, V = 100 cubes
7 L = 5 mm, D = _____ mm, H = 3 mm, V = 75 cubes
8 L = _____ cm, D = 10 cm, H = 1 cm, V = 200 cubes
9 L _____ m, D = 2 m, H = 2 m, V = 400 cubes
10 L = 8 mm, D = _____ mm, H = 3 mm, V = 120 cubes

Set C

Find the volume in cubes of the following rectangular prisms given the lengths (L), depths (D) and heights (H).

1 L = 4 cm, D = 2 cm, H = 1 cm, V = ________

2 L = 8 cm, D = 2 cm, H = 1 cm, V = ________

3 L = 4 cm, D = 2 cm, H = 2 cm, V = ________

4 L = 5 m, D = 4 m, H = 1 m, V = ________

5 L = 4 m, D = 3 m, H = 2 m, V = ________

6 L = 10 m, D = 2 m, H = 1 cm, V = ________

7 L = 5 mm, D = 4 mm, H = 3 mm, V = ________

8 L = 10 cm, D = 10 cm, H = 1 cm, V = ________

9 L = 10 m, D = 6 m, H = 2 m, V = ________

10 L = 8 mm, D = 5 mm, H = 2 mm, V = ________

Set D

Circle the greater volume of water.

1 110 mL or 1 L

2 0.1 L or 110 mL

3 1 L or 900 mL

4 1010 mL or 1.1 L

5 0.5 L or 50 mL

6 1000 mL or 2 L

7 2.5 L or 3000 mL

8 $\frac{1}{2}$ L or 60 mL

9 $3\frac{1}{2}$ L or 3000 mL

10 10 000 mL or 9 L

Set F

1 How many individual cubes would be in a larger 10 x 10 x 10 cube? ________

2 What would the volume of a cube with side lengths of 3 units be? ________

3 If a box was 2 cm long, 2 cm deep and 2 cm high, what would its volume be? ________

4 How much would half a litre of water weigh? _____

5 At 20 L per minute, how much water goes onto a lawn in 20 minutes? _____

6 The volume of a rectangular prism equals length + width + height. True or false? _____

7 Could the volume of a room possibly be 110 square metres? _____

8 Find the volume of a 4 x 4 x 4 unit cube. ________

9 When you carry a 10 L bucket that is half full of water, you carry _____ kg of water.

10 My bedroom is 3 m long, 3 m wide and 2 m high. The room's volume is _____ cubic metres.

Measurement and Geometry

Unit 27 Time: Digital and analogue conversions

Both digital and analogue (or sweep-hand) clocks are used in our everyday lives so you need to be accurate with both timing methods. Remember that a.m. means ante meridiem and deals with times before noon; p.m. means post meridiem and deals with times after noon.

Set A

Change these into sweep-hand times.

1 7:17 ______________________

2 5:35 ______________________

3 10:23 ______________________

4 1:54 ______________________

5 6:47 ______________________

6 2:58 ______________________

7 12:14 ______________________

8 4:34 ______________________

9 8:49 ______________________

10 9:21 ______________________

Set D

How many minutes from:

1 **7:55 to 8:05?** ______

2 **12:20 to 1:00?** ______

3 **3:55 to 5:05?** ______

4 **8:12 to 10:12?** ______

5 **6:14 to 7:13?** ______

6 **2:24 to 3:25?** ______

7 **9:40 to 11:00?** ______

8 **8:20 to 10:05?** ______

9 **5:55 to 7:05?** ______

10 **4:44 to 5:04?** ______

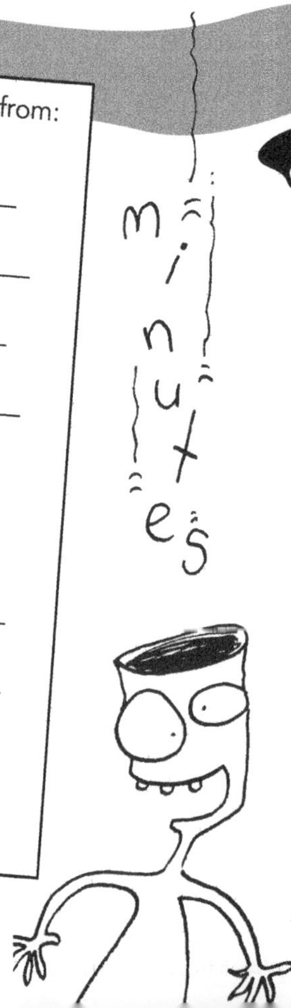

Set E

How many hours from:

1 1 a.m. to 11 a.m.? ______

2 2 a.m. to 10 a.m.? ______

3 5 a.m. to 12 noon? ______

4 9 a.m. to 3 p.m.? ______

5 7 a.m. to 7 p.m.? ______

6 8 p.m. to 7 a.m.? ______

7 4 a.m. to 5 p.m.? ______

8 7 a.m. to 1 p.m.? ______

9 2 p.m. to 1 a.m.? ______

10 5 a.m. to 4 a.m.? ______

Set B

Change these into digital times.

1 12 minutes past 8 ______
2 10 minutes to 4 ______
3 22 minutes past 3 ______
4 12 minutes to 6 ______
5 a quarter past 11 ______
6 a quarter to 9 ______
7 4 minutes to 10 ______
8 16 minutes to 8 ______
9 23 minutes past 1 ______
10 11 minutes to 7 ______

Set C

How many minutes from:

1 10 minutes to 5 to 5 minutes past 5? _____
2 8 minutes to 11 to 2 minutes past 11? _____
3 a quarter to 6 to a quarter past 6? _____
4 11 minutes to 9 to 11 minutes to 10? _____
5 20 minutes past 4 to 21 minutes past 5? _____
6 1 minute to 9 to 1 minute past 10? _____
7 28 minutes past 2 to 28 minutes to 3? _____
8 20 minutes to 11 to 20 minutes past 11? _____
9 3 minutes to 12 to 3 minutes past 1? _____
10 6 minutes to 3 to 6 minutes to 5? _____

Set F

1 The album I played started at 10:20 and lasted for 70 minutes. It finished at ____________.

2 School lasts for 7 hours, starting at 8:40 a.m. and ending at ____________.

3 Is 12:00 a.m. noon or midnight? ____________

4 I flew north for 3 hours, starting at 11:30 p.m. and landing at ____________.

5 The game started at 12 minutes to 5 or, digitally, at ____________.

6 The 90-minute movie began at 9:34 and finished at ____________.

7 Suva is 2 hours ahead of Sydney, where it is currently 11:55 a.m. In Suva it is currently ____________.

8 New York is 12 hours behind Sydney. In New York it is 9 p.m. and in Sydney it is ____________.

9 I must tape a TV show at 1:35 p.m., or at 25 to 2 in the ____________.

10 Breakfast lasted from 8:55 until 12 past 9, a duration of ____________ minutes.

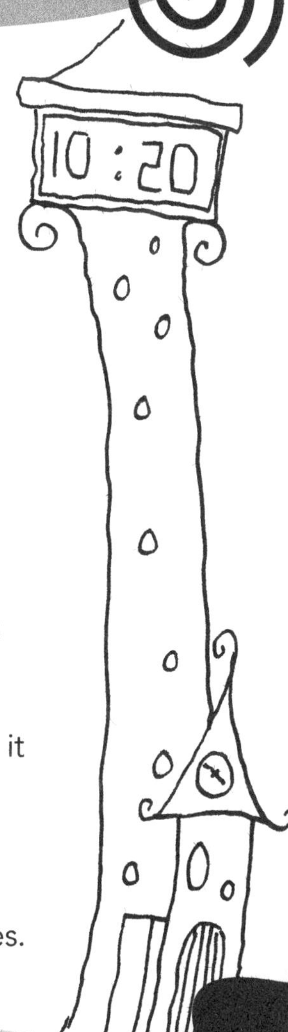

Measurement and Geometry

Unit 28
Time: Unit equivalences

Time can be split into units as small as a second and as large as a millennium. See how well you can move from one unit to another in these exercises!

Set A

What fraction of an hour are the following times?

1 30 minutes ☐
2 15 minutes ☐
3 45 minutes ☐
4 10 minutes ☐
5 20 minutes ☐
6 40 minutes ☐
7 50 minutes ☐
8 5 minutes ☐
9 55 minutes ☐
10 1 minute ☐

Set B

What fraction of a year are the following durations?

1 1 month ☐
2 3 months ☐
3 9 months ☐
4 11 months ☐
5 1 week ☐
6 13 weeks ☐
7 1 fortnight ☐
8 13 fortnights ☐
9 3 terms ☐
10 1 semester ☐

Set E

How many days in:

1 March + April? ________
2 May + June? ________
3 August + September? ________
4 October + November? ________
5 December + January? ________
6 winter? ________
7 spring? ________
8 autumn? ________
9 summer (non-leap year)? ________
10 summer (leap year)? ________

Set C

What day of the week will it be:

1 7 days after Wednesday? ___________

2 7 days before Friday? ___________

3 13 days after Thursday? ___________

4 13 days before Monday? ___________

5 16 days after Sunday ___________

6 28 days before Saturday? ___________

7 7 fortnights after Tuesday? ___________

8 72 days after Monday? ___________

9 76 days before Friday? ___________

10 778 days after Saturday? ___________

Set D

What month comes:

1 2 before January? ___________

2 4 after May? ___________

3 6 after September? ___________

4 6 before September? ___________

5 11 after June? ___________

6 11 before December? ___________

7 12 after March? ___________

8 26 after October? ___________

9 145 after July? ___________

10 145 before February? ___________

Set F

1 What is 10 days after 30 May? ________

2 What is the smallest possible number of Tuesdays in any year? ________

3 Which two consecutive months in the same year have the same number of days? ______________________

4 Which two consecutive months, not in the same year, have the same number of days? ______________________

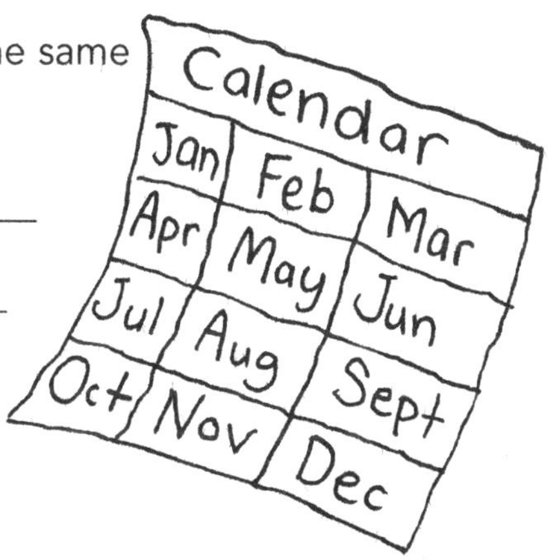

5 What is the greatest number of Fridays in any month? ________

6 How many 2 hour movies could you watch in a day? ________

7 How many days from 11/6/2006 to 1/7/2006? ________

8 How many days from 11/7/2008 to 1/8/2008? ________

9 How many days from Christmas Day to New Year's Day? ________

10 How many fortnights in a standard February? ________

Number and Algebra

Unit 29 Money: Making amounts, addition and subtraction

Making amounts of money economically means using the smallest number of notes and coins possible. Remember to always start with the most valuable note or coin. Adding and subtracting with money uses the same method as for 2-digit decimals. Look for shortcuts when dealing with amounts like $9.95.

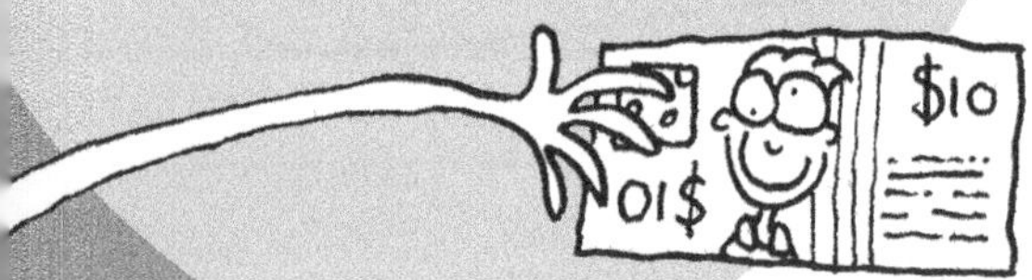

Set A

How many coins would be required to make, as quickly as possible, the following amounts of money?

1 **45 cents** ☐
2 **60 cents** ☐
3 **80 cents** ☐
4 **$1.25** ☐
5 **$1.70** ☐
6 **$2.30** ☐
7 **$4.90** ☐
8 **$6.50** ☐
9 **$8.75** ☐
10 **$12.40** ☐

Set B

How many notes would be required to make the following amounts of money as quickly as possible?

1 **$55.00** ☐
2 **$80.00** ☐
3 **$95.00** ☐
4 **$105.00** ☐
5 **$135.00** ☐
6 **$225.00** ☐
7 **$360.00** ☐
8 **$490.00** ☐
9 **$555.00** ☐
10 **$980.00** ☐

Set E

What change from $100.00 would I receive if I spent:

1 $5.00? ________
2 $5.85? ________
3 $8.00? ________
4 $8.75? ________
5 $9.75? ________
6 $19.95? ________
7 $28.00? ________
8 $28.90? ________
9 $47.00? ________
10 $47.65? ________

Set C

How many notes and coins would be required to make the following amounts of money as economically as possible?

1	$6.70	
2	$9.90	
3	$12.30	
4	$18.85	
5	$23.35	
6	$78.00	
7	$98.80	
8	$123.20	
9	$174.45	
10	$199.95	

Set D

Find the totals of the following amounts of money.

1 **50 cents + 20 cents + 40 cents** ________

2 **$4.00 + $6.00 + $12.00** ________

3 **$11.50 + $13.50** ________

4 **$22.00 + $23.80** ________

5 **$43.60 + $9.95** ________

6 **$28.70 + $9.95** ________

7 **$84.85 + $9.95** ________

8 **$9.95 + $9.95** ________

9 **$75.00 + $99.00** ________

10 **$231.55 + $99.00** ________

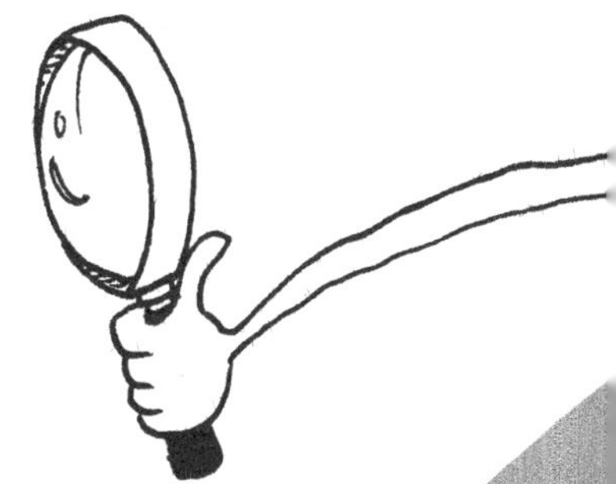

Set F

1 The total of one of each of the six available coins in our money system would equal $_____.

2 The total of one of each of the five available notes in our money system would equal $_______.

3 Which note has the greatest surface area? __________

4 Which note has the third-greatest surface area? __________

5 Which note is predominantly green? __________

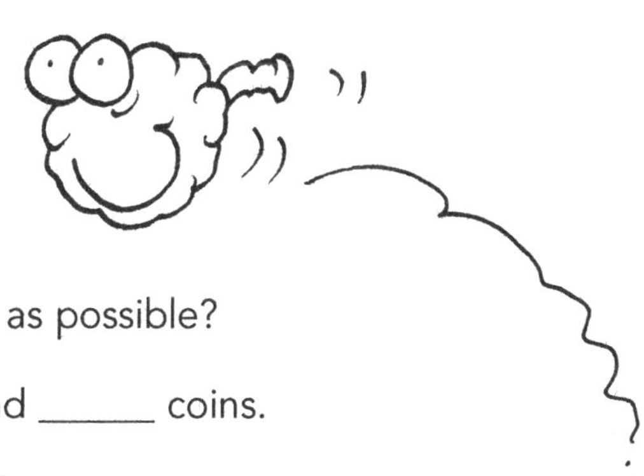

6 How many coins are required to make $4.55 as economically as possible?

7 My new shoes cost $79.00. I should pay with ______ notes and ______ coins.

8 $19.00 can be made using _______ coins as quickly as possible.

9 How many coins would be needed to make $3.20 as uneconomically as possible? ___________

10 Can $200.00 be made with one example of every note and coin in our money system? ______

Measurement and Geometry

Unit 30
2D and 3D: Properties and directions

Two-dimensional shapes, called polygons, are flat and can be drawn easily on a piece of paper. Three-dimensional objects, called polyhedra, have depth and can be picked up.

North, south, east and west are the four main points of the compass with directions between these points referred to by their joined names, such as north-west and south-east.

Set A

Which polygon, or polygons, are used to make the following polyhedra?

1 **cube** ______________________
2 **square pyramid** ______________________
3 **rectangular prism** ______________________
4 **cylinder** ______________________
5 **hexagonal pyramid** ______________________
6 **triangular prism** ______________________
7 **hexagonal prism** ______________________
8 **pentagonal prism** ______________________
9 **pentagonal pyramid** ______________________
10 **tetrahedron** ______________________

Set B

How many polygons are needed to make the following polyhedra?

1 **cube** ____
2 **cylinder** ____
3 **tetrahedron** ____
4 **rectangular prism** ____
5 **triangular prism** ____
6 **square pyramid** ____
7 **pentagonal pyramid** ____
8 **pentagonal prism** ____
9 **hexagonal pyramid** ____
10 **hexagonal prism** ____

Set E

How much of a turn, and in which direction, is the fastest way from:

1 north to west? ______________________
2 south to north? ______________________
3 east to west? ______________________
4 south to east? ______________________
5 north to south? ______________________
6 north to east? ______________________
7 south to west? ______________________
8 east to south? ______________________
9 east to north? ______________________
10 north-west to south-east? ______________________

Set C

Which direction is opposite to:

1 north? ________

2 west? ________

3 south? ________

4 east? ________

5 north-west? ________________

6 south-east? ________________

7 north-east? ________________

8 south-west? ________________

9 a quarter turn right of north? ________

10 a quarter turn left of north? ________

Set D

Which directions are adjacent to:

1 north-west? ____________________

2 south-west? ____________________

3 east? ____________________

4 south? ____________________

5 north-east? ____________________

6 north? ____________________

7 south-east? ____________________

8 west? ____________________

9 a half turn from east?

____

10 a half turn from north-east? ____________________

Set F

1 How many rectangles can be found on a triangular prism? ____________________

2 An ice-cream is a hemisphere on top of a ________.

3 To the north of South Australia is ____________________.

4 A square pyramid contains ____________________ triangles.

5 A tetrahedron has ________ faces.

6 Perth is ________ of Sydney.

7 A half turn from south-east is the direction ____________________.

8 A full turn from east is ________.

9 When closed, this book is the shape of a ____________________.

10 A billiard ball is an example of a ________.

Statistics and Probability

Unit 31
Chance: Concepts of likelihood

The likelihood of something happening is the chance of it occurring. This can be said using words such as 'possible' or 'certain'. It can also be said as a fraction, like 3/10, which we read as '3 out of 10' or as a decimal such as a 0.3 chance.

For these sets of questions, imagine that you have 30 cards numbered 1 to 30. Cards 1 to 10 are red, cards 11 to 20 are white and cards 21 to 30 are blue. Shuffle the cards and have them face down.

Set A

How many cards are:

1 even? ____
2 odd? ____
3 red? ____
4 bigger than 12? ____
5 smaller than 25? ____
6 between 13 and 28 inclusive? ____
7 blue and even? ____
8 white and bigger than 20? ____
9 red and even? ____
10 blue and odd? ____

Set B

Is the chance certain (C), likely (L), 50/50, unlikely (U) or impossible (I) of drawing a card that is:

1 a 9 ______
2 Odd ______
3 Blue or red ______
4 11 to 24 ______
5 1 to 19 ______
6 Red ______
7 Black ______
8 1 to 30 ______
9 11 to 30 ______
10 15 to 27 ______

Set E

Answer 'true' or 'false' to the following statements.

1 The chance of drawing a red card is the same as for a blue card. ______
2 The chance of drawing an even card is the same as for a white card. ______
3 The chance of drawing an odd card is the same as for a blue or red card. ______
4 The chance of drawing a red card is the same as for a red even card. ______
5 The chance of drawing an odd card, as a decimal, is 0.5. ______
6 The chance of drawing a card under 30 is certain. ______
7 The chance of drawing a 1, 3, 4, 7 or 9 white card is zero. ______
8 The chance of drawing a 1, 2, 3, 4 or 30 is the same as for drawing a 1, 2, 3, 4 or 29. ______
9 The chance of drawing an 8, 9 or 10 card, as a decimal, is 0.1. ______
10 The chance of drawing a 15 card is only half the chance of drawing a 30 card. ______

Set C

Which has the better chance of being drawn?
(Answer 50/50 if the chance is equal.)

1 A card less than 15 or an odd numbered card ________

2 An odd card or a red card ________

3 An even card or an odd card ________

4 A 6 or a 29 ________

5 A card bigger than 15 or a card smaller than 15 ________

6 A card bigger than 10 or a card smaller than 21 ________

7 An odd white card or an even blue card ________

8 A card bigger than 15 or a blue card ________

9 An odd red card or an even white card ________

10 A red 11 or a blue 22 ________

Set D

What is the chance of drawing (answer as a fraction in simplest form):

1 a card numbered 30? ____

2 a card numbered 1, 2 or 3? ____

3 an even number? ____

4 an odd number? ____

5 a blue card? ____

6 a white card? ____

7 a card bigger than 10? ____

8 an even blue card? ____

9 an odd red card? ____

10 a red or a white card? ____

Set F

1 How many of the 30 cards have three letters in their number name? ____

2 What is the chance of drawing one of these cards, as a fraction in simplest form? ____

3 How many of the 30 cards have more than three letters in their number name? ____

4 What is the chance of drawing one of these cards, as a fraction in simplest form? ____

5 How many cards are red and do not have three letters in their number name? ____

6 What is the chance of drawing one of these cards, as a fraction in simplest form? ____

7 How many of the white and blue cards are even-numbered cards? ____

8 What is the chance of drawing one of these cards, as a fraction in simplest form? ____

9 How many cards, greater than 15, are white? ____

10 What is the chance of drawing such a card, as a fraction in simplest form? ____

Revision

Unit 32 Revision: All sorts

Here are some revision questions that will cover all of the things you have worked through since Unit 1.

Good luck!

Set A

1 50 + 13 = ☐

2 37 + 21 = ☐

3 80 – 34 = ☐

4 67 – 25 = ☐

5 9 x 6 = ☐

6 12 x 9 = ☐

7 45 ÷ 5 = ☐

8 121 ÷ 11 = ☐

9 240 ÷ 12 = ☐

10 10th multiple of 7 = ☐

Set B

1 30 x 50 = ______

2 1, 2, 3, 6 are factors of ____

3 Double 26 ____

4 Half of 83 ____

5 6 and six zeroes = ________

6 23,507 to nearest 100 _____

7 Find $\frac{1}{3}$ of 27 ____

8 $\frac{12}{48}$ in simplest form ____

9 $\frac{13}{100}$ = 0.____

10 0.7 + 0.02 = ____

Set E

1 Find the lowest common multiple of 4 and 6. ____

2 How many factors does 13 have? ____

3 Double 12 and double it again. ____

4 What is half of half of 60? ____

5 What is one less than one hundred thousand? _______

6 Round 78 498 to the nearest 1000. _______

7 $\frac{1}{4}$ equals the decimal ____.

8 0.8 – 0.4 + 0.2 = ____

9 Find the 7th term: 1, 2, 4, 8, . . . ____

10 7 x 7 – 11 + 12 = ____

Set C

1 76, 68, 60, 52 Rule = ____

2 4 x 5 ÷ 10 + 3 = ___

3 0.7 m = ____ cm

4 7.5 kg = ______ g

5 8 L = ______ mL

6 4:36 in analogue time ________________

7 June is in the season of ________

8 40 mm x 40 mm = __________________

9 ______ 5 cent coins = 65c?

10 A brick's shape __________________

Set D

1 17 + 180 = ☐

2 24 + 73 = ☐

3 140 – 34 = ☐

4 87 – 45 = ☐

5 7 x 3 = ☐

6 9 x 8 = ☐

7 30 x 400 = ☐

8 $\frac{55}{5}$ = ☐

9 Divide 84 by 7 ☐

10 $\frac{360}{6}$ = ☐

Set F

1 Find the perimeter of a square with side lengths of $3\frac{1}{2}$ metres. ____

2 Area = length x width x height. True or false? ______

3 4 litres of water weighs ____.

4 A 10 cm sided cube has a volume of ______ cubic centimetres.

5 April + September = ____ days.

6 From 4 p.m. to 1 a.m. is ____ hours.

7 $4.00 – $2.55 = ______

8 All pyramids contain ________________.

9 All prisms contain ________________.

10 Tossing a head is a ________ chance.

Glossary

Add	To group together
Adjacent	Next to
Altogether	The answer to an addition problem
Analogue clock	A sweep-hand clock
Autumn	March, April, May
Bi	A prefix meaning 2
Centi	A prefix meaning 1/100
Centimetre	100th of a metre
Century	100 years
Composite	A number with more than two factors
Day	24 hours
Deca	A prefix meaning 10
Decade	A period of 10 years
Decagon	A 10-sided shape
Difference	How far one number is away from another number
Divide	To split up into equal pieces or to share
Dodecagon	A shape with 12 sides
Double	To add a number onto itself
Dozen	12
Duration	How long something lasts
Edge	A boundary
Equilateral	Sides the same length
Equal difference	Subtraction sums with the same answer, like 12 – 3 and 11 – 2
Face	A side of a 3D shape
Factor	What divides into a number
Fortnight	14 days
Gram	The standard unit for mass
Groups of	Counting in lots
Halve	Divide into two equal parts
Hemisphere	Half a sphere, like a scoop of ice-cream
Hendecagon	A shape with 11 sides
Heptagon	A shape with 7 sides
Hexagon	A shape with 6 sides
Hour	60 minutes
Kilo	A prefix meaning 1000
Kilogram	1000 grams
Kilometre	1000 metres
Leap year	A year of 366 days
Litre	The standard unit of capacity
Margin	How far two numbers are apart
Metre	The standard unit of length
Millennium	1000 years
Millilitre	One-thousandth of a litre
Minute	One-sixtieth of an hour
Month	One-twelfth of a year
Multiples	The answers to times tables
Multiply	Count groups
Nonagon	A shape with 9 sides
Octa	A prefix meaning 8
Octagon	A shape with 8 sides
Penta	A prefix meaning 5
Pentagon	A polygon with 5 sides
Perimeter	The length of the boundary of a shape
Polygon	A 2D shape with many corners
Polyhedra	A 3D shape with many faces
Prime	A number with just two factors
Product	The answer to a multiplication problem
Quad	A prefix meaning 4
Quadrilateral	A 4-sided shape
Quadruple	To multiply by 4
Quotient	The result of a division question
Regular (shape)	Having the same side lengths
Remainder	What is left over after a division sum has been completed
Remove	To take away
Rhombus	A 4-sided figure with equal sides but no right angles
Right angle	An L-shaped angle of 90 degrees
Round	To take a number to the nearest 10, 100, 1000 etc.
Rule	The pattern in a sequence
Season	A quarter of a year
Second	One-sixtieth of a minute
Semester	Half a year at school
Sequence	A number pattern
Share	To divide into equal pieces
Simplest form	To write a fraction using the smallest numbers possible
Solve	To find the answer to a question
Sphere	A 3D shape like a ball
Spring	September, October, November
Subtract	To take away
Sum	The answer to an addition problem
Summer	December, January, February
Term	Each member of a sequence
Term	One quarter of a year at school
Tessellate	To fit together without leaving gaps
Times	Groups of
Total	The answer to an addition problem
Tri	A prefix meaning 3
Triple	To multiply by 3
Twice	2 times, or to double
Vertex	The corner where lines meet on 2D or 3D shapes
Week	7 days
Winter	June, July, August
Year	365 days